LAST WORDS, FOR WAR

STATEMENTS OF THE SYMBIONESE LIBERATION ARMY

Last Words, For War: Statements of the Symbionese Liberation Army

This compilation first published in 2022 by Warcry.

ISBN 978-1957452012

This compilation © 2022 by Warcry

For information, submission guidelines, bulk requests, or general inquiries, please contact:

peter@peteryoung.me

Also published by Warcry:

The A.L.F. Strikes Again: Collected Writings Of The Animal Liberation Front In North America (Animal Liberation Front)

Animal Liberation Front: Complete US Diary Of Actions

Liberate: Stories & Lessons On Animal Liberation Above The Law (Peter Young)

Flaming Arrows: Collected Writings of Animal Liberation Front Activist Rod Coronado (Rod Coronado)

From Dusk 'til Dawn: An Insider's View of the Growth of the Animal Liberation Movement (Keith Mann)

Underground. The Animal Liberation Front in the 1990s (various)

INTRODUCTION

The so-called Symbionese Liberation Army rose into world renown on the basis of two crimes.

The fact that murder, even socially adjusted murder, is among the Bay Area norms, gives special interest to the marvelous success of the SLA in getting and keeping its audience. Never before has so little crime bought so much fame.

The triumph of the Symbionese in this respect developed from a set of isolated potentials cleverly put together by SLA theoreticians, and thoroughly recorded in their letters and other documents. In these writings the SLA provided something for every appetite. In killing the loved and admired Black educator, Marcus Foster, and killing him on the maxim that he was a traitor to his race, they elicited not only horror, but widespread discussion and challenge. In kidnapping Patricia Hearst, a pretty young heiress, and holding her hostage in some unimaginably secret headquarters, they added responses of sex, sentiment, and class, to those of caste and race. These crimes alone, once admitted or claimed, would have brought them into the limelight for a week or two, especially in the excitable communities around the Bay. But by their literary programs the SLA writers carried their renown much farther.

Delivered one by one, carefully, to the media, the SLA documents forced the constitutional and philosophical identity of the SLA into the consciousness of thoughtful people, and successfully presented the SLA soldiers as friends and benefactors to thousands or tens of thousands of such Bay Area people as manage to believe that good things can be had for nothing.

Here as elsewhere, the SLA got much result from little input. Even if the Hearst food program had proceeded at the grandiose level in which the SLA first envisaged it, the costs it would have involved would not have equaled the sums spent in a single day for the regular social and welfare operations in California. But the food program completed the SLA publicity program, adding the curiosity and admiration of people who could be reached by no other means. If earlier deeds and words had earned the attention of intellectuals, sensation-hunters, and responsible citizens, the new deed with free food added the attention of the dispirited, calloused, and cynical. Thus the whole society, from top to bottom, was drawn in.

The catholic appeal of the SLA, projected through its writings as well as its deeds, grew out of the catholic make-up and broad literary experience of its personnel. Two highly volatile elements joined in its creation. One of these consisted of young or youngish social reformers, the children of prosperous middle-class families, students or graduates of good universities, and veterans of heavy talk and moderate action in the late 1960's, the golden age of youthful militancy. They had enjoyed wide publicity and wide acceptance as members of the anti-Vietnam movement, and afterwards gone off into clusters and constellations of lesser movements, for love, for greening, for mild drugs, for price-control and rent-control, for the head-counting kinds of equality, for acceptance of homosexuals, hiring of women, and so on. Very importantly, they had gone into theories of law and penology, and reached the conclusion that every prisoner in every jail was a victim of society rather than an enemy of it. As their documents show, they thought of all prisoners as political prisoners, referred to the prisons of California as concentration camps, and described all police as political police. For some or most of them, the notion of reform was bedded intimately with the notion of violent action. Their early thoughts in the direction of prisons consequently became thoughts about helping prisoners to escape.

The other salient faction in the SLA is even more definable. Its nucleus was formed by two Black men, both scions of self-respecting Black families, both bright and literate, both criminals with long records, both escapees from the California prison system. Through them a few other Blacks, including Black women, were attracted to the movement. Though not the originators of the SLA, these Black men and criminals, with their better experience of real violence and terror, were arbitrarily denominated its leaders. Eventually their dominance in the making of SLA documents brought to these a language and philosophy especially directed towards Black have-nots, and it was to Blacks and Black organizations that they mainly looked as their supporters and allies. To the organization, these men brought a new simplicity, narrowness, and one-sidedness of image and idea. Text prepared by them often reads parallel to the literature of Black-oriented consciousness groups.

SLA members were not workers in any Marxist or Maoist sense. In honesty, the SLA made scarcely any claim to represent the workers, but only "the people", "the poor", and other groups defined only by a putative victimization. Here was developed an early weakness. As a California organization, the SLA was obliged to make an appeal to Spanish-Americans as well. But in California, just as in the Latin nations, Spanish-American militancy has been keyed to real working-class concerns. As represented by the Venceremos of California and other western states, radical Chicanos cleave to the classic Socialist and Syndicalist patterns of European tradition, and demand tight goals and reasonable tactics. The dream-ridden SLA appeal to this important minority was consequently hopeless from the first.

The clientele of the SLA was expanded beyond Blacks and Chicanos by means of umbrella clauses meant to cover every minority or pseudo-minority which has captured public attention in recent years. The intimacy between the interests of the SLA and the interests of the mass media is well demonstrated by this paralleling of clients. As summed up in Screed 4, given below, SLA clients and potential allies include Asian, Black, Brown, Indian, White, Women, Gray, and Gay, the last two terms signifying the old and the homosexual. In the food program originally envisaged by the SLA, and described by them in Screed 15 and other documents, food recipients would include all people who could show "welfare cards, social security pension cards, medical cards, food stamp cards, disabled veteran cards, parole or probation papers, and jail or bail release papers. Over five million Californians, the majority, not minority, of California adults, would thus have been beneficiaries of the Robin Hood part of the SLA program.

As Black organizations, and a few others, rallied round to help with the Hearst food program, they generated wide publicity of their own. By early March, the food program and the arguments which accompanied it were more important to the newspapers and electronic media than the kidnapping, while the murder of Foster was totally lost in history and seldom mentioned at all. Attempts to get public attention back to the issues of politics and terror were made by the SLA, and forlornly by the still-captive Patricia Hearst herself. Screeds 19 and 20, with their headnotes, record these efforts. But except for terror and free food, there was little in the SLA program that was capable of attracting admiration, or even continuing attention, from any broad public. Most articles of the program recorded in the screeds represented the ordinary desiderata of a prosperous and civilized society, and could have been promulgated as easily by General Grant as by General Cinque. In the Bay Area, home of so many manifestos, it seemed like only one more of the same.

But that is not the last word, for the successes of the SLA have brought into question the ability of society to react and repress. Mature participants in American movements thought radical in their time have profited from the ability of American society to accept slow and measured changes, and by its concomitant ability to resist opportunities of quicker change through violence and coercion. Our radicals have been protected from violence at the small cost of eschewing violence themselves. The responsible thought and stable laws of the nation have conditioned all their progress. But the equations brought into play by the SLA criminal and publicity programs seem to be skewed in a different way. To many, it has almost seemed that the venom of the seven cobra heads was real, and that it poisoned all the thought and the law which it touched.

The media also collapsed in the face of the SLA threats. A newspaper blackout began at once, settling down to the refusal of Bay Area editors, not only of papers but also of radio and television, to publish any kind of opinion or comment on the events, either by their own personnel or by their clients and readers. Soon the SLA domination of the media was total. Early in the game, in Screed 11, spokesmen of the SLA threatened to "execute" any person who aided law enforcement officers, or the FBI, or who criticized the SLA program in the media, or who refused to print exactly what the SLA sent them, a successful coercion which peaked in their demand that the two "comrade soldiers" accused of the murder of Marcus Foster be presented to America on nation-wide television. The media performed as directed, and proved itself no match for the dozen or so young outlaws of the SLA.

In the absence of leadership and the blackout of educated comment, the people of the Bay Area generated whispers and rumors of all kinds. Such rumors still arise and spread, and will undoubtedly continue to get credence until responsible voices are dominant again, and the society with its laws resumes its orderly functions. And what are these whispers, these rumors? In many of the Black communities it is currently believed that either Steven Weed or Patricia Hearst, or both, engineered the kidnapping and were accessories to the murder. It is generally thought, perhaps by a majority of all races, that the police and FBI learned the whereabouts of Patricia Hearst at the beginning. Embroidery beyond that belief is complex, for many reasons are assigned to the failure of the police to go and get her back. In one line of thought, the police feared that the death of Miss Hearst in such an attack would be blamed on them; in another, they were afraid of uprisings in Berkeley and in Black neighborhoods, where many voices and many graffiti presented the SLA and its Marshal Cinque as saviors of the race The notion that the SLA was established as an agent-provocateur arm of the FBI itself is widespread among young radicals in Berkeley and the Haight-Ashbury, with other locales of that genus. And on the simplest level, the failure of the food giveaway to work smoothly was blamed on the FBI, the police, the Hearsts, and others. In this theory, the riots and thefts which occurred on giveaway days were deliberately staged to provide bad press publicity for Black people, or "the people", or "the poor". This line of thinking was taken in several Screeds by SLA spokesmen and in Screed 20 by Patricia Hearst herself, but it was common on the streets before the screeds were written.

The most important of the beliefs that swept through the articulate circles of the Bay Area was, however, the belief that the terrorist formulas actually worked, that they produced quick and useful results, and that society and its laws had no way of countering them. And this amounted to a belief in terror itself as a mode of politics. Thus the Symbionese had an early success beyond their wildest dreams.

SCREED ONE

COMING OF THE COBRA

The following communication was mimeographed on the back of paper sheets bearing the cobra illustrations on their fronts. It consolidates and improves upon historical and parapsychological accounts of the cobra symbol in common reference books.

One of its interesting features is the shifting values which it gives for the "seven principles" shown by the seven heads. Two are printed in this single screed, and others replace them in screeds that follow. One may suspect that the original decision to use a cobra with seven heads for a major emblem arose from the fact that there were seven original Symbionese Federation or SLA members.

The talismanic importance of this screed to the SLA leadership is shown by the fact that the "Court of the People" adjudged its failure to be printed at once in Hearst newspapers and other media to be proof of malicious bad faith on the part of the "Hearst Empire" and "fascist AmeriKKKa" generally.

The emblem of the Symbionese Liberation Army is 170,000 years old, and it is one of the first symbols used by people to signify God and life. The two bottom heads on each side of the Cobra represent the four principles of life: the sun, the moon, the earth, and the water. The three center heads represent God and the universe, and are called the God head. The number seven as embracing all the universal forces of God and life can be traced to the Egyptian temples and their seven pillars, to the seven candles of the pre-Zionist, North African religions, to the Buddhist and Hindu religions, and to the North and South American Indian religions. This is because the seven principles explain the interrelationships of life, of the family and the state, of the human anatomy and the universe. And because the basic principle behind any kind of union and series of relationships must be equally accessible to all concerned, we see why the seven heads of the cobra have but one body. The thoughts and purpose in each of the seven heads of the cobra penetrates its common body and soul, and from this we see how the source of the cobra's survival lies not in any individual head, but rather in the relationship and unity of all the heads to each other.

The Symbionese Liberation Army has selected the Seven Headed Cobra as our emblem because we realize that an army is a mass that needs unity in order to become a fighting force, and we know that true unity among people must be based upon a concern that is universal. It is a revolutionary unity of all people against a common oppressor enemy of the people. This unity of seven heads in one body defines the essence of co-operation and socialism in the great undertaking of revolutionary war. Through the puritan capitalist ethics of competition, individualism, fascism, racism, sexism, and imperialism the enemy is attacking us. This enemy functions by means of attacking one race or group among us in an attempt to force us into submission and division and isolation from each other. From these attacks, we have learned that our common enemy will not stop until we come together to stop him, for he lives off the murder and oppression of our divided and therefore defenseless people.

We have chosen the Seven-Headed Cobra as the emblem of the S.L.A. because our forces are from every walk of life, from every religion, and of every race, and by our unity does our strength and our common goal for freedom from the chains of capitalism make true the meaning of our seven principles of unity. Our military and political strength arises from the masses of all our people, for when the people are at one in their inmost body, they shatter even the hardest of iron or of bronze, and when the people understand each other in their inmost heart, their words are sweet and strong.

The seven memberships of our federation are men and women who are black, brown, yellow, red, white, young and old. Each of these members joins together and speaks and fights for the best interests of all within the body, just as one head of the cobra can not be attacked without the others rising to strike with venom in self-defense to destroy the attacker. Each head of the cobra stands in organic need of all the others in order to maintain its survival.

From this example of the necessity of unity in order to survive, the S.L.A. will build and fight for the socialist unity of all oppressed peoples. A cry from any one of us will echo in the body of our common ear [sic], and we will attack out of instinct, and in self-defense, for our survival. And with the venom of our seven heads we will destroy the fascist insect who preys upon the life of the people; and with the minds of our seven heads, and the spirit of our one body and soul, we will secure a future for our children.

SCREED TWO

COBRA HEADS

The plate on the facing page reproduces the main Symbionese visual symbol, complete with its listing of values purportedly underlying activities of the SLA. The chart was put together by means of scissors, paste, and Xerox at some unknown time, but probably in the early summer of 1973, at the Berkeley Public Library.

In consideration of the Black emphasis of the SLA, the pride of place, and of large print, was given to Swahili terms culled from a dictionary. The likelihood that any member of the SLA understood Swahili is small indeed, but "courses" in Swahili were a much-advertised feature of the California educational scene in the 1960's, and some Blacks retain a vague belief in the concept that Blacks, like Germans or Russians, ought to have a traditional mother-tongue. The Chinese characters painstakingly cut out and pasted on are a salute to the large and still growing Chinese population of California. The semantics of the seven terms, and the rational use of them, belong wholly to Western languages and the Western revolutionary dialectic.

It was intended by the Symbionese leadership that the symbol and headings become part of the collective consciousness of "the poor" or "the people." Significantly, one of the first demands of Patricia Hearst's kidnappers was that "the document... shall be placed in newspapers and other forms of the media in its exact form, not omitting any area." The symbol was also to be displayed wherever the Hearst free food was distributed. During February 1974, the symbol was sprayed on walls in Black areas of many Bay Area cities. But it is a hard symbol for untrained hands to draw successfully, and soon gave way to the mere initials SLA, or slogans such as "Right On, Sin Cue," and "SLA is OK."

KUJICHAGLIA
La Libre Determinación
Self Determination

KUUMBA
Creatividad
Creativity

UJAMAA
Producción Cooperativa
Cooperative Production

UMOJA
La Unidad
Unity

UJIMA
Trabajo Colectivo Y Responsabilidad
Collective Work And Responsibility

IMANI
Fe
Faith

NIA
Propósito
Purpose

SCREED THREE

THE SLA OATH

The seven values listed on the basic cobra-head chart were carefully explicated in a seven-part oath or vow. From internal evidence one may judge that the oath was developed as a committee project, rather than by a single intelligence.

Its insistence on the elements of pride, morale, and solidarity unmistakably connect the oath to the Black Studies and Black Awareness programs of the 1960's, and to the other Consciousness and Awareness programs (for Orientals, Hispanics, Prisoners, Women, Children, Homosexuals, and so on) which spun off from them. Collations with oaths and programs of Latin terrorist groups, in particular the Tupemaros, and with non-terrorist quasi-revolutionary groups such as the Venceremos of California, also reveals an indebtedness. Copies of the documents were circulating along Telegraph Avenue in Berkeley in early 1973, and others came to light immediately after the assassination of Marcus Foster in November. That it was circulated in other places, including prisons, is certain.

It seems likely that the term "nation" in items 1, 3, 5, and 7 was substituted for an earlier term indicating race or caste, and that the non-revolutionary concept of environmentalism under "KUUMBA" was added in consideration of the "ecology" movement which engrossed public attention in the period 1968-70. Very noticeable is its concentration on the Federation aspect of Symbionese activity, and its failure to mention the "Army" or militant aspect.

In its apparently final form, the oath was sent to Radio Station KPFA and the Hearst family with the demand that it be published in "all public media".

TO THOSE WHO WOULD BEAR THE HOPES AND
FUTURE OF OUR PEOPLE, LET THE VOICE OF
THEIR GUNS EXPRESS THE WORDS OF FREEDOM

UMOJA - LA UNIDAD UNITY To strive for and maintain unity in our household, our nation and in The Symbionese Federation.

KUJICHAGULIA - LA LIBRE DETERMINACION - SELF-DETERMINATION -- To define ourselves, name ourselves, speak for ourselves and govern ourselves.

UJIMA - TRABAJO COLLECTIVO Y RESPONSABILIDAD - COLLECTIVE WORK AND RESPONSIBILITY --- To build and maintain our nation and the federation together by making our brothers' and sisters' and the Federation's problems our problems and solving them together.

UJAMAA - PRODUCCION COOPERATIVA -- COOPERATIVE PRO-

DUCTION -- To build and maintain our own economy from our skills, and labor and resources and to insure ourselves and other nations that we all profit equally from our labor.

NIA PROPOSITO - PURPOSE -- To make as our collective vocation the development and liberation of our nation, and all oppressed people, in order to restore our people and all oppressed people to their traditional greatness and humanity.

KUUMBA - CREATIVO -- CREATIVITY -- To do all we can in order to free our nation and defend the federation and constantly make it and the earth that we all share more beautiful and beneficial.

IMANI -FE - FAITH -- To believe in our unity, our leaders, our teachers, our people, and in the righteousness and victory of our struggle and the struggle of all oppressed and exploited people.

Screed Four

CONSTITUTION AND PROGRAM

The constitutional document of the Symbionese group is also the production of a committee or convention rather than a single intelligence. Though dated August 21, 1973, it was undoubtedly put together earlier, and from documents of other organizations made at a still earlier time. It was among the writings found by the police after the Concord house occupied by Russell Little, David Remiro, Nancy Ling Perry, and others was set afire. The text below is from the typescript released to Radio Station KPFA and the Hearst family after the kidnapping of Patricia Hearst.

When it arrived at KPFA, the document was enjambed with the document called "Goals of the Symbionese Liberation Army", published below as Screed 5. But evidence of tone and style, as well as much overlapping and some minor contradictions, show that it was composed at a different time, and at meetings dominated by a different mood. Evidence of grammar shows, moreover, that it was originally prepared as the controlling vehicle of the Symbionese Federation, and that references to the Symbionese Liberation Army were added later. Readers sensitive to English prose style will note jarring inconsistencies of skill and tone among the preparers of the document, and conclude that at least two, and possibly three, documents were drawn into the single pandect. It was in the process of this assembly that the militant and terrorist aspect of Symbionism came to the fore.

Other differences which the document embodies, and perhaps harmonizes, are those between Black and Integrated policies, and American and International policies. The insistence upon "Black and minority leadership" in the first paragraph points to a date after the Berkeley street kids had been joined by the escaped Black prisoners. As elsewhere in the screeds, appeals are made to all social fractions which have recently elected to define themselves as abused and thwarted. The appeal to "Asian, Black, Brown, Indian, White, Women, Grey, and Gay" is hopeless as Left practical politics, since the fractions are irreconcilable except within a broadly defined constitutional democracy such as the U.S.A. But the SLA was only following the media.

In this document is the seed of a slightly different but much more important dialectical problem which keeps recurring in later screeds of the Symbionese. In the second paragraph, the writers insist that their Federation is "NOT A GOVERNMENT": in the third paragraph they insist that it is "NOT A PARTY". What then is it? Later attempts to establish a positive identity indicate a philosophical tangle well illustrated by the mystifying assertion that the SLA is "made up of members of all the people". The confusion was perhaps intended: it is important for a Federation which claims to constitute mankind to leave room open for all mankind to claim membership in it.

The forensic result of the confusion is also advantageous. Since the "enemy" is identified mainly by slogans and maxims, and never really defined, and the Federation people are defined mainly as the victims of this enemy, the principle of militancy is reduced to action alone. As Prince Kropotkin liked to point out, it is always impossible for such dilemmas to be settled except through simple medium of revolutionary violence.

THE SYMBIONESE FEDERATION & THE SYMBIONESE LIBERATION ARMY DECLARATION OF REVOLUTIONARY WAR & THE SYMBIONESE PROGRAM

August 21, 1973

The Symbionese Federation and The Symbionese Liberation Army is a united and federated grouping of members of different races and people and socialist political parties of the oppressed people of The Fascist United States of America, who have under black and minority leadership formed and joined The Symbionese Federated Republic and have agreed to struggle together in behalf of all their people and races and political parties interest in the gaining of FREEDOM and SELF DETERMINATION and INDEPENDANCE for all their people and races.

The Symbionese Federation is NOT A GOVERNMENT, but rather it is a united and federated formation of members of different races and people and political parties who have agreed to struggle in a UNITED FRONT for the independance and self determination of each of their races and people and The Liquidation of the Common Enemy. [sic, for all spellings.]

And who by this federated formation represent their future and independant pre-governments and nations of their people and races. The Symbionese Federation is NOT A PARTY, but rather is a Federation, for its members are made up of members of all political parties and organizations and races of all the most oppressed people of this fascist nation, thereby forming unity and the full representation of the interests of all the people.

The Symbionese Liberation Army is an army of the people, and is made up of members of all the people. The S.L.A. has no political power or political person over it that dictates who will fight and die if needed for the freedom of our people and children, but does not risk their life or fight too for our freedom, but rather the S.L.A. is both political and military in that in the S.L.A. the army officer, whether female or male, is also the political officer and they both are the daughters and sons of the people and they both fight as well as speak for the freedom of our people and children.

The Symbionese Federation and The Symbionese Liberation Army is [sic] made up of the aged, youth and women and men of all races and people. The name Symbionese is taken from the word symbiosis and we define its meaning as a body of dissimilar bodies and organisms living in deep and loving harmony and partnership in the best interest of all within the body.

We of the Symbionese Federation and The S.L.A. define ourselves by this name because it states that we are no longer willing to allow the enemy of all our people and children to murder, oppress and exploit us nor define us by color and thereby maintain division among us, but rather have joined together under black and minority leadership in behalf of all our different races and people to build a better and new world for our children and people's future. We are a United Front and Federated Coalition of members from the Asian, Black, Brown, Indian, White, Women, Grey and Gay Liberation Movements.

Who have all come to see and understand that only if we unite and build our new world and future, will there really be a future for our children and people. We of the People, and not the ruling capitalist class, will build a new world and system. Where there is really freedom and a true meaning to justice and equality for all women and men of all races and people, and an end to the murder and oppression, exploitation of all people.

We of the Symbionese Federation and The S.L.A. are the children of all oppressed people, who have decided to redefine ourselves as a Symbionese Race and People. Yet, recognizing the rich cultures of each and enforcing our rights to existance [sic] of our many cultures within a united federation of indep…pendant and sovereign nations, each of them flourishing and protected by its own laws and codes of self determination.

We are of many colors, but yet of one mind, for we all in history's time on this earth have become part of each other in suffering and in mind, and have agreed that the murder, oppression, and exploitation of our children and people must end now, for we all have seen the murder, oppression and exploitation of our people for too long under the hand of the same enemy and class of people and under the same system.

Knowing this, the Symbionese Federation and The S.L.A. know that our often murderous alienation from each other aids and is one of the fundamental strengths behind the ruling capitalist class's ability to murder and oppress us all. By not allowing them to define us by color, and also recognizing that by refusing ourselves to also internalize this false division definition[sic], knowing that in mind and body we are facing the same enemy and that we are all comrades of one people, the murdered and oppressed, we are now able to become a united people under the Symbionese Federation and make true the words of our codes of unity that TO DIE A RACE, AND BE BORN A NATION, IS TO BECOME FREE.

Therefore, we of the Symbionese Federation and The S.L.A. DO NOT under the rights of human beings submit to the murder, oppression and exploitation of our children and people and do under the rights granted to the people under The Declaration of Independance of The United States, do now by the rights of our children and people and by Force of Arms and with every drop of our blood, Declare Revolutionary War against The Fascist Capitalist Class, and all their agents of murder, oppression and exploitation. We support by Force of Arms the just struggles of all oppressed people for self determination and independance [sic] within the United States and The World. And hereby offer to all liberation movements, revolutionary workers groups, and peoples organizations our total aid and support for the struggle for freedom and justice for all people and races. We call upon all revolutionary black and other oppressed people within the Fascist United States to come together and join The Symbionese Federation and fight in the forces of The Symbionese Liberation Army.

SCREED FIVE

GOALS OF THE SYMBIONESE

The list of goals or objectives of the Symbionese is a more skillful and coherent document than the constitutional one given in Screed 4. Before the burning of the Concord home used as headquarters by the Information Unit of the SLA, the list was unknown. A copy of it was picked up by police among the ashes, and a full transcript was placed in the kit of communications sent to Station KPFA and the Hearst family in February. This transcript is from the photocopy of the original document.

There are not many errors. Moreover, there are few or none of the specifically Black expressions which occur in other documents of the SLA. And in addition, this screed contains flourishes which, though often vague and trite, indicate a real concern for efficient and evocative English. Taken together with the ideas described in the fourteen separate articles of the document, these facts tell us a good deal about the main author. We can take it that this author was a white person, probably a female, certainly college-educated, coming from a literate middle-class background, and the veteran of years of bloodless reformism and revolutionism in radical student circles of Telegraph Avenue or the Haight-Ashbury. She has enough mental capacity to avoid the circlings and overlapping endemic among SLA writers; she keeps theory and fact appropriately separated; alone among her SLA colleagues, she has mastered the rudiments of philosophic abstraction.

The items she lists as "goals" offer a flagrant testimony about the plethora of social issues which have chased one another across the American mind in the past decade. Only half of them are revolutionary or political in any traditional sense. Others take up pensions (8), marriage (9), child-care centers (11), "ecology" (13), the rent-control ideas adored in university and Black circles at Berkeley and elsewhere (14), and the rule of love and "meaningful relationships" which was so much mooted in the age when hippies painted flowers on their autos and we spoke of "flower children". Reading the list, we seem to be reviewing the history of university and press liberalism from 1962 to 1972.

Though there are plenty of references to warfare and struggle among the sixteen "goals" on the list, the emphasis of the document as a whole is peaceful enough. It belongs to the literature of protest rather than the literature of revolution, and undoubtedly speaks of the time when the Federation was more important than the Army. The pedantic list of "five basic needs of life" given in the concluding paragraph is from a school textbook. The slogan which follows it ("If the quest for freedom") is unknown elsewhere.

THE GOALS OF THE SYMBIONESE LIBERATION ARMY

1. To unite all oppressed people into a fighting force and to destroy the system of the capitalist state and all its value systems. To create in its place a system and [ie, of] sovereign nations that are in the total interest of all its races and people, based on the true affirmation of life, love, trust, and honesty, freedom and equality that is truly for all.

2. To assure the rights of all people to self determination and the rights to

build their own nation and government, with representatives that have shown through their actions to be in the interest of their people. To give the right to all people to select and elect their own representatives and governments by direct vote.

3. To build a people's federated council, who will be a male and female of each People's Council or Sovereign Nation of The Symbionese Federation of Nations, who shall be the representatives of their nations in the forming of trade packs [ie, pacts] and unified defense against any external enemy that may attack any of the free nations of the federation and to form other aids to each others' needs.

4. To aid and defend the cultural rights of all the sovereign nations of The Symbionese Federation, and to aid each nation in the building of educational and other institutions to meet and serve this need for its people.

5. To place the control of all the institutions and industries, of each nation into [sic] the hands of its people. To aid sovereign nations of the federation to build nations where work contributes concretely to the full interest and needs of its workers and the communal interest of its communities and its people and the mutual interest of all within the federation of nations.

6. To aid and defend the rights of all oppressed people to build [sic] nations which do not institute oppression and exploitation, but rather does institute the environment of freedom and defends that freedom on all levels and for all of the people, and by any means necessary.

7. To give back to all people their human and constitutional rights, liberty, equality and justice and the right to bear arms in the defense of these rights.

8. To create a system where our aged are cared for with respect, love, and kindness and aided and encouraged to become assets in their own ways to their nations and to their communal community. That the life that moves around them is not a frightening and murderous one and where life is not a fear, but rather one of love and feeling and of unity.

9. To create a system and laws that will neither force people into nor force them to stay into [sic] personal relationships that they do not wish to be in, and to destroy all chains instituted by legal and social laws of the capitalist state which acts as a reinforcing system to maintain this form of imprison-

ment.

10. To create institutions that will aid, reinforce and educate the growth of our comrade women and aid them in making a new true and better role to live in life and in the defining of themselves as a new and free people.

11. To create new forms of life and relationships that bring true meanings of love to people's relationships, and to form communes on the community level and bring the children of the community into being the responsibility of the community, to place our children in the union of real comradeship and in the care and loving interest of the revolutionary community.

12. To destroy the prison system, which the capitalist state has used to imprison the oppressed and exploited, and thereby destroy the love, unity, and hopes of millions of lives and families. And to create in its place a system of comradeship and that of group unity and education on a communal and revolutionary level within the community, to bring home our daughters and sons, and sisters and brothers, fathers and mothers, and welcome them home with love and a new revolutionary comradeship of unity.

13. To take control of all state land and that of the capitalist class and to give back the land to the people. To form laws and codes that safeguard that no person can own the land, or sell the land, but rather the nations' people own the land and use it for their needs and interest to live. No one can own or sell the air, the sky, the water, the trees, the birds, the sun, for all of this world belongs to the people of this earth.

14. To take controls [sic] of all buildings and apartment buildings of the capitalist class and fascist government and to totally destroy the rent system of exploitation.

15. To build a federation of nations, who shall formulate programs and unions of actions and interests that will destroy the capitalist value system and its other anti-human institutions and who will be able to do this by meeting all the basic needs of all of the people and their nations. For they will be all able to do this because each nation will have full control of all of its industries and institutions and does not run them for profit, but in the full interest of all the people of its nation.

16. To destroy all forms and institutions of Racism, Sexism, Ageism, Capi-

talism, Fascism, Individualism, Possessiveness, Competitiveness and all other such institutions that have made and sustained capitalism and the capitalist class system that has oppressed and exploited all of the people of our history.

By this means and the mutual aid and unity of each nation within The Symbionese Federation, will each nation be able to provide to each person and couple and family free of cost the five basic needs of life, which are food, health care, housing, education and clothing, and in this way allowing people to be able to find and form new values and new systems of relationships and interests based on a new meaning to life and love.

IF THE QUEST FOR FREEDOM IS DEATH
THEN BY THE DEATH OF THE ENEMY WILL BLACK AND OTHER
OPPRESSED PEOPLE FIND AND REGAIN THEIR FREEDOM

Screed Six

WAR COUNCIL ALLIANCE

The purpose of the sixth document is to delineate a system by which "war" activities of the SLA can be usefully supported by other radical groups. The writing embodies a dogmatic, declarative, absolute style, uncertain grammar, and many bureaucratic and military terms. Some of its materials are probably drawn from manifestos of other revolutionary groups. Though it bears marks of committee thinking, it was surely written under direction of one presiding mind. My transcript of the SLA typescript preserves all errors except for obvious typos.

The document seems to anticipate the assassination of Marcus Foster, and was probably pulled together during the tense period when the leadership of the Symbionese passed from the "federation" to the "army". Both as a working plan to create alliances and as a guide to conducting them once established, it demonstrates experience and intelligence. It ably introduces a situation in which the SLA accepts equality of effort and honor among all violent organizations even while maintaining its supremacy over them.

There is a shadowy intimation that fellow-travelling organizations will be headed by Blacks The statement in Clause 9 that organizations may not join the War Council until they have had a "combat action" is believed by many people to have a relationship to unexplained ritual killings in the Bay area, and in particular to the coordinated killing of four whites on San Francisco streets on the night of January 30, 1974. The parable of the hand and fingers is drawn from a celebrated speech of Booker T Wathington in 1897 one of the staples of Black Studies programs for many years. In that speech, Booker T. Washington used the "hand" to represent all races together and the "fingers" each race.

The stipulation that all delegations to the "War Council" be of "two persons, one female and one male (if possible)" is drawn from a major preoccupation of the Americans today. In several places, including Clause 12, one learns the penalty for activities adjudged in conflict with the aims of the "War Council". It is significant that people who dropped away from the Symbionese movement when the Federation yielded preeminence to the Army have refused to help the authorities or inform the press.

There is little evidence to show that the "War Council" in its strictly warlike function received important support from other groups. The brilliant success of the SLA in the Foster killing and Hearst kidnapping produced a somewhat different constellation. Collectively named "the coalition", a dozen small organizations, all political and militant, all either Black or Black-dominated, permitted themselves to be lined up as supporters and monitors of the Hearst food giveaway program. Many of these groups are identified in Screed 15 and Screed 17, below. As noted in the headnote to Screed 4, the identity of the "enemy" is never clearly established. For this reason, the concept of "combat action against the enemy" as the prerequisite for alliance with the SLA is of fluid definition.

THE UNITED SYMBIONESE WAR COUNCIL TERMS OF MILITARY/ POLITICAL ALLIANCE

Our commitment to the revolutionary struggle for self-determination for all oppressed people and races and the international proletarian revolution is total and fully uncompromisable. Therefore, any relationship the Symbionese War Council has with any group or organization is based on their active military/political commitment to the goal of gaining freedom for all oppressed people and races.

1. Our alliance with any group or organization is based upon their firm decision to fight as well as talk in behalf of the people's interest, and once this commitment is clear then we can come together in order to:

   1. collectively develop a common strategy
   2. work together to develop tactical co-ordination
   3. Assist each other in developing the abilities and talents of all the members of the Symbionese War Council and to analyze the strengths and weaknesses of the leadership in order to constantly better all aspects of the ability and actions of the War Council, and its individual leadership from other organizations.

2. Command positions of The War Council are subject to the approval of all members of the council, based upon the military/political thinking and ability of the presented officer to work with others in the interest of freedom for all people and races.

3. Command positions in The War Council are not appointed by [whom] one knows, one's sex, one's color or the group or organization one belongs to, but only by one's Courage, Determination, intelligence, Aggressive Initiative and Capability as a Leader, and one's Military/Political thinking.

4. All members of The War Council are expected and fully are responsible for the military political leadership of The S.L.A., they must fight and speak for the people and this must be understood clearly by all members.

5. No member of The War Council can elect or select himself or herself to a position such as the head of a government or people's council; the War Council is totally an alliance OF WAR AGAINST THE COMMON ENEMY. The people themselves shall have and hold the ONLY RIGHT to select and elect their governments and government heads of state.

6. It is NOT the policy of The War Council to rip off [ie, steal] leadership or membership from other organizations, but rather it is the policy of The War

Council to aid and support the development and education of leadership to fulfill truly its responsibility to the people, and to allow the collective intelligence, leadership and resourcefulness of the leadership from different organizations and groups to flourish together and grow together; thereby forming an area where the collective interests and needs as well as weaknesses and strengths of each can benefit each IN THE COMMON STRUGGLE TO LIQUIDATE THE COMMON ENEMY.

7. A successful military force is a necessity for actualizing political goals and must therefore be held as a priority; therefore, the true assistance in the supplying of military equipment, materials, finances, personal [ie, personnel] is of the utmost importance, once these forces have fully committed themselves to open and total warfare against the common enemy and members of The War Council must understand this clearly.

8. Leadership of any group or organization who is truly committed and in agreement with the goals of the S.L.A. and the terms of military/political alliance may be presented to The War Council; however, the presented officer's membership is not confirmed until it is verified that prior to presentation for membership a combat action has been taken part in by that group, or organization within the last 12 months.

9. Once The War Council collectively agrees to an action or plan of strategy then that action shall be understood as an action of the S.L.A., and not of any single group or organization. Just as the fingers cannot call themselves a fist, and the fist cannot call itself the fingers. From time to time the membership on the War Council may disagree upon a particular action or strategy. When in disagreement, that particular membership need not participate in The S.L.A. action, but membership on The War Council is maintained only as long as all commitments made to the collective Symbionese War Council are continued to be fully adhered to.[sic] It is the disagreeing group or organization's responsibility to, on its own, prove out their ideas in order to change or modify its own or the collective War Council's direction.

10. It is the policy of The War Council not to involve itself in the internal political affairs or disagreements that may result within different organizations or groups. However, The War Council recognizes and accepts membership to the Council of any military/political unit, cell or organization that qualifies and shall recognize them as true representatives of that particular organization or group. It is the collective policy of The War Council that the failure of the

elected leadership to take her or his revolutionary responsibility as far as the War Council is concerned shall be totally the responsibility of the elected leader and not that of The War Council.

11. Organizations or groups that wish to serve in combat units must select two persons, one female and one male (if possible), who have full responsibility and authority to act and represent their group or organization and who will hold a command position in the unified command of The United Symbionese War Council.

12. All members of The Symbionese War Council must clearly understand that our commitment is total and our goal is the total freedom of the people and children and the destroying totally of the common enemy. Therefore, it is held that any restraining of supplies or other war materials etc. for political reasons or reactionary reasons or political chess games with the enemy, by any officer or other persons in the War Council, that by its actions endangers the lives of the women and men of The Symbionese Liberation Army shall be held as a full and total violation of this alliance pact and compromising with the enemy and the freedom and life of the people and children and therefore is punishable by death.

TO THOSE WHO WOULD BEAR THE HOPES AND FUTURE
OF THE PEOPLE, LET THE VOICE OF THEIR GUNS
EXPRESS THE WORDS OF FREEDOM.

SCREED SEVEN

SLA AND SUPPORT UNITS

Screed 5 follows closely upon Screed 4. Both are "military-political"; both deal with "tactical support" of the SLA by outside revolutionists; both take their tone from a single intelligent and sagacious organizing mind.

Persons experienced in activist activity will sigh in sympathy with the central paragraph of the document, where the writer effectively proposes that those who organize should organize "in support of something", and should eventually "do something" as well. The document reflects experience with tin-horn groups of the jail-lawyer and Telegraph Avenue types, where talk tends to lead to nothing except more talk.

The first and final paragraphs, where "egotistic opportunists and lovers of the group and organization" are indicted, reflect current enmity to the "star-trip" or "ego-trip" leadership of earlier organizations such as the Weather People and the Black Panthers.

TACTICAL SUPPORT UNITS

Each cell of The SLA TACTICAL SUPPORT UNITS is composed of elements of other organizations and groups and Individuals Under the strategy of The S L A it is totally impossible to follow the egotistic aspirations of many leaders of political organizations, since they continue to organize new organizations every time one falls apart, when they fail to understand that the people always organize to fight the enemy; and when leaders fail to start the fight, then the people fall from that organization.

To continue in this manner is totally reactionary, egotistic, Opportunist and anti-revolutionary, since to do so only allows for the continued grouping and regrouping of the same revolutionary people for the fight that never comes and with the only purpose of Organizing.

This is totally anti-revolutionary for within the true purpose of revolution there is [sic] only TWO DEEP PURPOSES: TO DESTROY THE ENEMY AND FREE THE PEOPLE. This in itself means the need for an army of the people that fights the enemy.

In order to organize, one must organize in support of something, one does not organize in support of having or belonging to or Just to organize, but rather one must have a purpose to organize around, and since in revolution it is the purpose to organize to fight the enemy and to support those that fight on the front lines, It is then clear that the people organize to fight and destroy the enemy. They do not organize to fight the enemy and then when it comes time to fight, claim that to fight the enemy will endanger the organization for this would show them to be lovers of positions and the organization and not true revolutionaries that love the people and children.

Since you as members of the people have organized to fight the enemy, for the reason that you are and do love the people, then it is clear to you where your true responsibility is, and that is to join and support those who are in the front lines fighting the enemy of us all, regardless of what color, group or organization they belong to, for the people are just this, they are not an organization or color or group, they are the oppressed, exploitated [sic] and the murdered, they are those we love and for whom we, if needed, are willing to die for, they are our children.

Therefore what is needed now is for you as lovers of the people to select in what area you are able and willing to fight in or give support to, either in the combat units or support units of The S.L.A., the choice is yours alone: to be and show yourselves as lovers of the people and our children and true to your word revolutionaries, or as egotistic opportunists and lovers of the group and organization and enemies of the people.

SCREED EIGHT

FOSTER MURDER AND COMMUNIQUE ONE

Dr. Marcus Foster, Superintendent of the Oakland school system, a Black man widely honored and admired, had come to California from a distinguished earlier career in the East. His chief assistant, Robert Blackburn, a white, had also served in other systems, and had spent some years in a Federal program organizing schools in Africa. Both had become involved in discussions about violence and murder in Oakland schools.

During the autumn of 1973, two particular suggestions, namely that police protection be given to teachers and students in schools, and that a system of voluntary identification be used to keep street kids and petty criminals off of school grounds, had been mooted in Board meetings. These measures had become issues of great importance to the Black communities in the East Bay. They were called discriminatory and anti-Black, and Board meetings at which they were discussed were generally violent. Foster and Blackburn supported only the second of the measures, and supported even that lukewarmly, but they failed to take the extreme positions demanded of them by radical Blacks.

As Screed 8 shows, the, moderation of these two men led to their being sentenced to death. On November 6, Election Night throughout the United States, the hit took place. As they walked from a School Board meeting to Blackburn's parked car, they were cut down by small-arms fire. Blackburn's wounds were from a shotgun, and after some time on the critical list he recovered from them. Foster was struck by eight pistol bullets, and died at once. Although this shooting occurred in series with a large number of other killings in the Bay Area, Dr. Foster's civic importance, wide public favor, and Negritude, made the murder a cause celebre throughout California and the nation generally.

This was the background for Communique No. 1, a "Warrant Order" claiming the honor, or onus, of the attack on Foster and Blackburn. The communique was sent to Radio Station KPFA, in Berkeley, a subscription FM station, culturally oriented but long identified with Black and other minority causes. Little notice was taken of the message, and it was thought a mere prank. However, its reference to "cyanide bullets" became important a few days later, when the Alameda County Coroner, in his report, stated that the bullets which killed Foster had been "drilled at their points and packed with potassium cyanide". From that time forward, the Symbionese Federation and the Symbionese Liberation Army were never out of the news.

A sharp degeneration of style and manner may be noticed in this communique as compared to earlier documents of the Symbionese. The difference is explained by the fact that after it surfaced in early December 1973, the SLA addressed the general public rather than its own people. Once vis-a-vis this broader audience, SLA writers adopted the persiflage techniques of ordinary admen. In their new mode, they shifted the semantics of their terms, added epithets likely to draw sympathetic reactions, and simply changed the names of things, as when the Oakland "Voluntary Identification Program" became "Forced Youth Identification Program."

The SLA reference to the death of Tyrone Guyton, and similar references in other communiques, is intended to show the SLA actions to be self-defensive. Tyrone Guyton was shot fleeing the police after a crime had been committed in Oakland. By many in the Black communities, he was adjudged a martyr and an illustration of tyranny and genocide.

SYMBIONESE LIBERATION ARMY

WESTERN REGIONAL YOUTH UNIT

Communique #1
Date: November 6, 1973
Warrant Order: Execution by Cyanide
Subjects: The board of Education, The Implementation of the Inter
nal Warfare Identification
Warrant Issued By: The Court of the People

Charges: Supporting and taking part in the forming and implementation of a
Political Police Force operating within the Schools of the People. Supporting
and taking part in the forming and implementation of Bio-Dossiers through
The Forced Youth Identification Program. Supporting and taking part in the
building of composite files for the International Warfare Identification Computer System.

Target: Dr. Marcus Foster, Superintendent of Schools, Oakland, California
Robert Blackburn, Deputy Superintendent, Oakland, California On the afore
stated date, elements of the United Federated Forces of The S.L.A. did attack
the Fascist Board of Education, Oakland, California, through the person of
Dr. Marcus A. Foster, Superintendent of Schools, and Robert Blackburn,
Deputy Superintendent.

This attack is to serve notice on the Board of Education and its fascist elements that they have come to the attention of The S.L.A. and The Court
of the People and have been found guilty of supporting and taking part in
crimes committed against the children and the life of the people.

This attack is also to serve notice on the fascist Board of Education and its
fascist supporters that The Court of the People have issued a Death Warrant on All Members and Supporters of the Internal Warfare Identification
Computer System. This SHOOT ON SIGHT order will stay in effect until
such time as ALL POLITICAL POLICE ARE REMOVED FROM OUR
SCHOOLS AND ALL PHOTO AND OTHER FORMS OF IDENTIFI-
CATION ARE STOPPED.

Indictment:

No. 1: The Board of Education has taken upon itself the roleforming and supporting a Special Political Police Force to and patrol the schools in our cities. The vast Black, D, Asian and conscious white youth communities of the Oakland-Berkeley area understand that this newest extension of surveilance is patterned after fascist Amerikan tactics of genocide, murder and imprisonment practice by Amerikan financed puppet governments in Vietnam, The Philippines, Chile and South Africa. We recognize that the school system censors and controls what we read, and that the Special Political Police Force is to censor and control what we say and do.

No. 2: The Board of Education has taken upon itself the role of forming and supporting the implementation of Bio-Dossiers through the Forced Youth Identification Program. The Photo Identification Program, with the additional composite files, is patterned after the system of apartheid in South Africa. The Bio-Dossiers classify our youth according to color and "criminal lencies" (will to be free) and seek to eliminate all our valiant freedom fighters by "relocating" (incarcerating) them to such concentration camps as Tehachapi Prison. Under the Preventative Act such concentration camps have the authority to incarate our youth from age of 15 for an "indefinite" period of time. The Preventative Crime Act stipulates that any youth displaying violent or "criminal" potential or the possibility of violent criminal potential in the future, in other words, any youth oppose the current system of censored Political Police-State education and seek to organize against it are to be classified as erous and either disarmed, shot, or imprisoned for expressing rights to be free, and defending the rights to freedom of their brothers and sisters.

3: The Board of Education has taken upon itself the role of)Orting and taking part in the implementation of the Internal Identification Computer System. The Internal Warfare I are based in the FBI's master computer system with information from the composite files of individuals who have expressed political views that may be regarded as differing from those of the fascist ruling class. Members of the liberation movements and organizations, as well as single individuals, are identified through photographs and bio-dossiers, supplied, in the case of our youth, by the Boards of Education and Public School Systems in our cities. The racist nature of the Internal Warfare Identification Computer System is clear since blacks and other minorities who refuse to serve the rich ruling class are automatically classified as potentially violent and "criminal". The CIA-ITT financed junta government in Chile uses similar bio-dossiers to murder all identified people who oppose the military takeover there or who do not serve and support the interest of the wealthy. Similar programs are carried out by governments financed by America and its military corporate enterprises throughout the word in the lands of the robbed; Vietnam, The Philippines, Chile, Brazil, Uruguay, South Africa are some prime examples.

The Black, Chicano, Asian and conscious White youth in our communities recognize the importance of the Oakland-Berkeley area to the liberation struggle of all oppressed people.

We know that the ruling class must seek to stop the revolutionary community here before the ruling class can regain its arm of control around the struggling and oppressed people of the world.

We understand that the definition of a fascist government necessitates the elimination of all who oppose its controls. We know that the school system does not educate us, but rather it lies to us in an attempt to perpetuate the interests of the rich ruling class. News of the successful liberation struggles of our brothers and sisters throughout the world is stifled because the enemy fears our knowledge of the fact that a truly determined people can never be defeated. We reject totally the ruling class values of personal material gain and competition among ourselves and we know that the enemy fears our understanding of the fact that nothing is more precious than freedom. The myth of a high-style superfly life and fashion show (a capitalistic rip-oft) does not sway us for we know that the fascist government of Amerika supplies the dope and the clothes and wants us to spend the rest of our lives paying for them. We are well aware that a fascist government will allow some of us to get high, while the rest of us go to concentration camps, and none of us are free.

It is clear that Dr. Foster and sideman, deputy superintendent Robert Blackburn, represent the rich ruling class and big business, and not the children and youth of our communities. The school system which they represent and serve does not teach us or address itself to the needs of our survival, but rather it does perpetuate the values of big business and the wealthy. Under the current system, the ruling class is educated to exploit, and our children and youth are educated to serve. We are not deceived by the superintendent and deputy. Robert Blackburn is a former director of education for the Peace Corps in East Africa. The Peace Corps, as well as AID, are promoted and financed as a front for the CIA, and have long been arms of American imperialist and racist oppression and genocide. Dr. Foster is a former member of the

Philadelphia Crime Commission, and now his advancement within the fascist process found him as initiator, promoter and supporter of Political Police Units armed with riot shotguns, to patrol our schools.

The Oakland-Berkeley area is considered potentially dangerous to American ruling class, that is why it has been selected for the Political Police Force within the Schools and the Forced Youth Identification Program.

Let it be known to those who sign for the implementation of these fascist programs, that the death of our manchild comrade youth, 14-year-old Tyrone Guyton, murdered on November 1st by three goons from the Emeryville Political Police Patrol, is NOT FORGOTTEN. Tyrone fell victim to the racist enemy who is instituting programs such as those initiated by Marcus Foster and Robert Blackburn aimed at control, imprisonment, execution and genocide of blacks and other minorities. Let it be known to those who sign for the implementation of these fascist programs that they sign their own death warrants. We of the black and other revolutionary youth communities have for too long seen the enemy prostitute our mothers, imprison our fathers, shoot our brothers and sterilize our sisters. We have learned the lesson; therefore, notice is hereby given on the enemy political police state and all its lackeys that we hold as an example to follow the courage of our slain comrade-in-arms Johnathan (George) Jackson and we call upon our mothers, fathers, sisters and brothers saying
*

TO THOSE WHO WOULD BEAR THE HOPES AND FUTURE OF OUR PEOPLE, LET THE VOICE OF THEIR GUNS EXPRESS THE WORDS OF FREEDOM.

DEATH TO THE FASCIST INSECT THAT PREYS UPON THE LIFE OF THE PEOPLE.

S.L.A.

SCREED NINE

THE FOSTER FOLLOW-UP

A few days after the death of Marcus Foster, the Oakland Board of Education voted not to deploy police advisors in the schools and not to institute the system of voluntary identification cards. The Board had continued to meet vigorous opposition from organizations of Blacks and other racial minorities, and may have yielded to these pressures more readily after the death of the moderate and intelligent Foster. Though filled with cyanide buckshot, Blackburn was still alive. In Communique No. 2, this time a mere 'Notification", the SLA "Court of the People" responded to both the new developments. Vaguely but unmistakably, it took credit for blocking the two security measures. And since its appeal was to uneducated and easily impressed people, it felt able to insinuate that Blackburn had either died with Foster or been kept alive by medical treatment available only to the "rich ruling caste".

SYMBIONESE LIBERATION ARMY
WESTERN REGIONAL YOUTH UNIT

Communique No. 2
Notification: Court Order
Subject: The board of Education, The Respecting of the Rights and Wishes of the People
Date: November 15, 1973
Order Issued By: The Court of the of the People

It has come to the attention of The Symbionese Liberation Army and The Court of the People that the fascist Board of Education has made an attempt to heed and respect the rights and wishes of the people by stating that they will not continue to take part in crimes committed against the children and the life of the people. Therefore, it is the decision of this court that the SHOOT ON SIGHT warrant issued November 6, 1973, be rescinded, and that all forces of the S.L.A. and the People's Army halt their attack on this aspect of the fascist enemy state. However, in the event that the fascist Board of Education does attempt to disguise their intentions and at any time reinstates programs of Political Police Forces in our schools, Forced Youth Identification cards, and contributions to the Internal Warfare Identification Computer System, then the Death Warrant Order is to be immediately reactivated without warning.

The Forces of The Symbionese Liberation Army commend people for their courage in refusing to fall prey to offers of bribery and rewards to be given for information which the enemy then use against the defenders of the people. We praise the spirit determination and strength of the vast Black, Chicano,

Asian and conscious white communities of the Oakland-Berkeley area, and remind the enemy rich ruling class that the people will always understand the effectiveness and tactics of revolutionary justice, and will never be deceived by the distortions and lies of the fascist news media. Marcus Foster has been likened to one of our slain leaders. We ask, who has ever heard of a Martin Luther King on the Philadelphia Crime Commission? Who has ever heard of a Martin Luther King having an aide who is a CIA agent, formerly acting as director of education for the Peace Corps in East Africa? We are all well aware that the fascist news media seeks to condition us by repressing the truth.

The people have seen no evidence to indicate that Deputy Superintendent Blackburn is in fact still alive. Traditionally, the fascist news media is quick to display photographs of members of enemy state who have managed to survive revolutionary justice and the will of the people. Usually we would see the enemy as he lays [sic] in his plush, private hospital room, while the wounds of oppressed people remain unattended. However, if Blackburn is alive, we, The Symbionese Liberation Army and The Court of the People wish to point out the contradiction between the medical care received by those who represent the rich ruling class, and that received by members of the poor and oppressed communities. It is obvious that medical technology does exist and that is a question of who receives the benefits of such care? Tyrone Guyton was shot down, handcuffed, and allowed to bleed to death in the gutter. For too long we have seen our people die from the enemy's bullets.

"DEATH TO THE FASCIST INSECT THAT PREYS UPON THE LIFE OF THE PEOPLE."

SCREED TEN

FAHIZAH'S LETTER TO THE PEOPLE

Along with other romantic stunts, for example the cobra symbolism and the "cyanide bullets", members of the SLA early opted for rebaptism with symbolic party names. The name of Cinque [pronounced Sin Kew] has become best known, but others such as Osceola, Bo, and Genina, keep cropping up in the documents. The name of Fahizah, the symbolism of which Fahizah herself explains, was the first to attain notoriety.

The Nancy Ling Perry who once wore the skin of Fahizah was a virtually perfect example of Berkeley street-radical. Born in an upper middle-class merchant family in a deluxe suburb of San Francisco, she became a high school live-wire, a cheer leader, and a sturdy worker for Barry Goldwater in the campaign of 1964. Her family were Quakers and she began her university career at Whittier College, the Quaker-sponsored school in Southern California whose best-known graduate is Richard Nixon. After a few semesters at Whittier she transferred her credits to the University of California at Berkeley, where she was an English major, an unsuccessful poet, and, very soon, a dedicated member of the Street People along Telegraph Avenue. Along the way she married, worked as a topless dancer, drew welfare payments, and rode the crest of the peace-oriented university movements of the 1960's. With the change of Telegraph Avenue styles, she, like other Street People, seems to have been left without a modish habitat or a popular mission.

From this relative emptiness, Nancy Ling Perry shifted her reformist attention to the affairs of Black prisoners. This concern had assumed great vogue in the years 1970 -72, and enjoyed regular stimulation through the saturation reporting of bloody events starring George and Jonathan Jackson, the Soledad Brothers, and Angela Davis, as well as the notable blood-feasts at San Rafael and San Quentin. With other young whites in the SLA, Nancy Ling Perry began a practice of visiting Black criminals in prison. These prison enterprises established the constellation of middle-class white youths and lower-class Black criminals which dominated the SLA in its year of fame.

In January of 1973, Fahizah, no longer a Ling or a Perry, inhabited a tract house at 1560 Sutherland Court in the dull East Bay town of Concord, near Berkeley. Russell Little, Joseph Remiro, and perhaps others, lived with her there. On January 10, Little and Remiro, driving near the house in a panel truck registered to her, were stopped by traffic patrolmen and elected to shoot it out with them rather than show their identification. Both were captured on the spot, uninjured. A few minutes later, neighbors of the house discovered it to be ablaze. Firemen and policemen who responded to the alarm discovered a cache of SLA literature, several maps and charts connected with the death of Foster, a couple of bombs, assorted small arms and ammunition, and cyanide of the kind used to make the "cyanide bullets" employed by the SLA. Fahizah, with three colleagues, had driven away at breakneck speed just before the fire was discovered.

Fahizah's testament is partly autobiographical, partly doctrinal, and partly exculpatory. Her letter reflects the concern, just shown in Screed 8, to maintain the image of the SLA as a successful and powerful revolutionary organization even in the face of temporary setbacks. In a half-earnest, half-jeering glissade at the end of her letter, Fahizah argues that the police discovered nothing of importance in the house on Sutherland Court. Many of her stipulations are merely quibbling, and some seem intended to block off criticisms of her from within the SLA itself. Nor does she bother to avoid far-fetched, even absurd, lines of argument. The SLA writers rely on the proposition that in the explosive atmosphere of class and race tension, discourse need not chain itself to the probable or even the possible.

The "August Seventh Movement" from which Fahizah struggles to dissociate the SLA is, or was, another Bay Area militant group. The August Seventh people have been thought to have killed a half-dozen whites for ritual reasons, and to have shot down a police helicopter, killing the pilot and his passenger. Claims had also been made to the effect that the August Seventh was responsible for the Foster-Blackburn shootings. The proposition that the August Seventh was an agent provocateur arm of the "Oakland and California State Political Police" is not supported elsewhere.

Fahizah xeroxed her letter and sent it to several newspapers and electronic-media stations, including KPFA. It was reported on, but not printed in full. It became important after the Hearst kidnapping had given the SLA its world-wide notoriety.

A LETTER TO THE PEOPLE

FROM FAHIZAH (former name nancy ling perry)

"TO THOSE WHO WOULD BEAR THE HOPES AND FUTURE OF THE PEOPLE, LET THE VOICE OF THEIR GUNS EXPRESS THE WORDS OF FREEDOM."

Greetings, my comrade sisters and brothers, all love, power and freedom to you. I am very glad to have this opportunity to speak to you, even though I know that what I am feeling cannot be completely expressed in words. You may have heard of me, not because I am any more important than any of you, but simply because my former name has been in the news lately. My name was Nancy Ling Perry, but my true name is Fahizah. What that name means is one who is victorious, and I am one who believes in the liberation and victory of the people, because I have learned that what one really believes in is what will come to pass. So, my name is Fahizah and I am a freedom fighter in an Information Intelligence Unit of the United Federated Forces of the Symbionese Liberation Army. I still am that, in spite of the fact that I am now being sought for a political action, and in spite of the fact that two of my closest companeros are now chained in the Adjustment Center (the prison's prison) at San Quentin concentration camp. I am still with other members of the SLA Information Intelligence Unit, and I am hiding only from the enemy and not from the people. I have no intention of deserting my commitment [sic] nor would I ever try to run away from it, because I have learned that there is no flight to freedom except that of an armed projectile. Although it is the practice of the Symbionese Liberation Army to act rather than talk, I am compelled to speak because I wish to make clear my position and why I am fighting, what it is I am fighting for, what the purpose and nature of the SLA information/intelligence unit is, and why I will continue to fight.

II

First of all, I think I should tell you something about my background and the evolution of my consciousness. Basically, I have three backgrounds: I have a work background, a love background, and a prison background. My prison background means that I have close ties and feelings with our in-carcerated brothers and sisters. What they have taught me is that if people on the outside do not understand the necessity of defending them through force of arms, then it is because these people on the outside do not yet realize that they are in an immediate danger of being thrown into concentration camps themselves, tortured, or shot down in the streets for expressing their beliefs. What my love background taught me was a whole lot of what love is all about, and that the greater one's capacity for love is, the greater is one's longing for freedom. What my work background taught me is that one of the things that every revolutionary does is to fight to get back the fruits of her or his own labor and the control of his or her own destiny.

When I was in high school in 1963-64, I witnessed the first military coup, against we [sic] the people of this country. I saw us passively sit by our TV.'s and unconsciously watch as the militarily armed corporate state took over the existing government and blatantly destroyed the constitution that some of us still believed in. I listened to the people around me deny that a military coup had taken place and claim that such a thing could not happen here. The people that I grew up around were so politically naive that their conceptions of a military coup only recognized those that have occurred in South America and African countries where the military and ruling class took over the government by an open force of arms. But the method of taking over the government was different here. Here the coup was simply accomplished by assassinating the then president john kennedy, and then assassinating any further opposition to the dictator who was to take power; that dictator is the current president richard nixon. In 1964 I witnessed these and other somewhat hidden beginnings of the military/corporate state which we now live in. And I heard my teachers and the government controlled media spread lies about what had happened. I saw the Civil Rights protests, the killings and bombings of my black brothers and sisters and the conditioned reactions of extreme racism in my school and home. When I questioned my teachers about how these occurrences related to the meanings of democracy and freedom that we were told existed to protect us all, the answer I got was that we were better off not knowing the truth about what was happening. I told my teachers and my family and friends, that I felt that we were all being used as pawns and puppets, and that those who had taken over the government were trying to keep us asleep and in a political stupor. I asked my teachers to tell me what happened in Nazi Germany; I asked them to tell me the meaning of fascism; I asked them to tell me the meaning of genocide; and when I began to hear about a war in Vietnam, I asked them to tell me the meaning of imperialism. The answer to all my questions then was either silence, or a reply filled with confusion and lies, and a racist pride and attitude that well, after all, it was all for us.

The experience of living in Amerikkka has since taught me the realities of what fascism, imperialism, and genocide mean; and I have discovered the truth about the military take-over and the police state dictatorship, not because I studied about it in college, but because I see it everyday, and because truth is something that is honestly known, as easily as beauty is seen. There is no need for me to relate here everything that I have seen, or everything that I am sure you are already aware of. I am sure, my sisters and brothers, that you realize that the government is now in the rapid and steady process of removing the means of survival from the lower class and giving these benefits to the middle class in an effort to rally support from them. And as the government is removing these means of survival from the people, then naturally the people who have been robbed must in turn take back what rightfully belongs to them, and take back what they need in order to survive. This the current dictatorship calls a crime, whether they take food from the grocery store, or take to the streets to make a speech, or take a gun in their hand to defend themselves.

As a member of the Symbionese Liberation Army information/intelligence unit. I fight against our common oppressor, and this I do with my gun as well as my mind. I try to use my mind and my imagination to uncover facts, so that when the SLA attacks it will be in the right place, and that the actions of the more experienced SLA combat units will truly serve to benefit the people and answer their needs. The action taken by the SLA combat unit in reference to the Oakland Board of Education was a specific response to political police state programs and the failure of the Board to heed the rights and demands of the people in the community. The specific program was one of the photo identification (similar to the system of apartheid in South Africa), biological classification in the form of bio-dossiers which classify students according to race and political beliefs, internal warfare computer files, and armed police state patrols within the schools. Intensely thorough intelligence operations carried out by one of the SLA information units was [sic] able to obtain factual information that Foster's signature was the first to appear on the Nixon Administration inspired proposal for armed police agents within certain Oakland schools and various forms of computer classification of students. Further intelligence revealed that Foster's background included membership on the Philadelphia Crime Commission. Foster's sideman, Blackburn, is a CIA agent. As director of Education in East Africa he worked to implement test programs against black people there, and he trained other agents to carry them out so that he could return to his country and introduce those same programs here. I feel a need to explain this again because I want to make it clear that the SLA was not indiscriminately issuing death warrants for Foster, Blackburn and anyone else, but rather we were attacking the programs and proposal of which they were the initiators, supporters and first signers. Such an attack was the only means left open to us to demand that the people's wishes be met, and that all such dangerous, genocidal programs be stopped.

The government controlled media has made some reference to the effect that this action was carried out by white people made up in black face. Members of the SLA do not have to make up in black face in order to defend the black community, since the SLA is a federation formed in the style of a revolutionary United Nations whose commanding leadership is composed of representatives of the black, brown, yellow, red and white communities. We have more than enough members from every race to carry out any operation. As revolutionaries we would never disguise ourselves by race, because we would never deliberately act in a manner that would bring further police investigation onto any one race of peoples [sic]. But I would like to ask, since when does one have to be black in order to care about the murder of 14 year old Tyrone Guyton by political police state death squads, since when does one have to be white in order to feel for the starving children in Appalachia, since when does one have to be Asian in order to care about stopping the napalming of children in Vietnam, since when does one have to be brown in order to fight against the mass slaughters being conducted by the military junta in Chile? ? ? ? Since when? ? ? ? Not since we have come to realize that we are all one in struggle.

III

I am a member of the Symbionese Liberation Army information/intelligence unit and that means that my responsibility is to aid the combat units with information, and keep myself armed at all times. I am in a race to learn how to fight, because I am in a race to survive. SLA information/intelligence units have a military/political alliance with SLA combat units. What that means is that information units totally support armed struggle. That is to say that all members of the SLA understand that politics are inseparable from struggle, in fact politics have no meaning without armed combat and information units to give politics a purpose.

The Symbionese Liberation army is unlike many existing Political organizations in this country which support the armed liberation struggles of peoples throughout the world, but when it comes to the struggle here in Amerikka, they [sic] consistently denounce militancy and revolutionary violence, and in so doing denounce the only means left to the people to achieve their liberation.

I believe that whenever people are confronted with oppression, starvation and the death of their freedom that they want to fight. It has been the history of many political leaders to suppress this will of the people, and to pretend that the people do not have the right to fight, and to pretend that the people will somehow achieve their liberation without revolutionary violence. But the truth is that there has never been a precedent for a non-violent revolution; the defenseless and unarmed people of Chile can testify to that. All members of the SLA recognize that we, right here in Amerikka are in a state of war, and that in a state of war, all must be armed, and understand the true meaning of self-defense. When any member of the people's army strikes out at the murderer of our people and children, we are doing so in self-defense, we are doing so because we are left no alternative, and force of arms is now our only legal means to affect revolutionary justice. However, the natural instincts of many people in our country have become perverted by the conditionings to which they have been subjected, they have been conditioned to be afraid of revolutionary violence. I no longer have these fears because as a comrade of mine named Osceola has taught me, "The only way to destroy fear is to destroy the makers of fear, the murderer and the oppressor". A revolutionary is not a criminal nor is she or he an adventurer, and revolutionary violence is nothing but the most profound means of achieving internal as well as external balance.

IV

I would like to correct and clarify the information given to you by the regime-controlled media and police-state reports associating the Symbionese Liberation Army with the August 7th. First of all, statements about August 7th literature and original communiques being found in the Concord house are completely untrue. The Symbionese Liberation Army is NOT the August 7th; in fact, the August 7th is a counter revolutionary Oakland City and California State police plot to discredit revolutionaries and confuse the people. Freedom fighters act only in the interest of the people, they do not unnecessarily shoot down a helicopter whose crashing would endanger lives of people in their communities, nor do they credit themselves with events or accidents that occur in which they had no part, nor do they issue threats which they are unprepared to carry out, nor do they expose the nature and whereabouts of their forces, as for example in the recent statement issued by August 7th saying that armed guerrilla units existed inside the prisons. The events and communiques associated with the August 7th served only enemy purposes: that is, a state wide lock-down went into effect in the prisons and the people began to think of revolutionary action as that which would endanger their lives and homes. As a member of the SLA I can tell you that the SLA takes full credit and responsibility for its actions, we acknowledge everything that we do, and if we had shot down a helicopter, we would say so; and if I had participated as a decoy in a taxi cab incident I would say so. However, I would like to tell you not to rely solely on my analysis that the August 7th and the Oakland and California State Political Police are one and the same, but instead, just take a look for yourselves. Ask yourselves of the extent to which the police state will go to discredit revolutionaries by labeling all street violence as revolutionary activity and by issuing nothing but threatening communiques and then saying that such threats were coming from revolutionaries. It isn't just coincidence that the week the August 7th issued an idle threat against the life of prison official Procunier, was the same week that the California legislature re-instated the death penalty.

V

The house in Concord, Calif. was a Symbionese Liberation Army information/intelligence headquarters, nothing more. The house was set on fire by me only to melt away any fingerprints that may have been overlooked. It never was intended that the fire would totally destroy the premises, because there was nothing left there that was of any real consequence to us, nor was there any material left behind that could stagnate the functioning ability of the SLA to carry on the struggle. The reports that mass armaments were found in that house is a lie. It is an attempt to frame my two Comrade brothers and it is an assertion to cover up the fact that there were no weapons found there. All that remained were 3 broken BB guns, a couple of malfunctioning gas masks, a few research books, and several liberation posters on the wall. Also, let me tell you that no one living or coming to that house was a part of the SLA combat forces. This can be easily verified; first of all, everyone in SLA combat forces is offensively armed with cyanide bullets in all weapons that they carry; and up until today this had NOT been the case for SLA information/intelligence units or any support units, at that time all units but combat were only defensively armed with hand guns and carried no cyanide bullets. Secondly, we can easily verify that the ballistics on the .38O now in the hands of pig agents do not match those of the weapon used in the attack on the Oakland Board of Education. Information/intelligence units or any support units were never allowed to possess or have any contact with combat unit weapons. Beginning January 11th however, a directive was issued by The SLA and The Court of the People stating that as of that date, all units of The Symbionese Liberation Army are to be heavily, and offensively armed with cyanide bullets in all their weapons. I would like to convey the word, to my 2 captured companeros: you have not been forgotten, and you will be defended because there has been no set back and all combat forces are intact.

There really are no words available to me to express what I feel about the capture of my two companeros. They are in a concentration camp now because none of us were offensively armed, and because I was not aware that they were under attack. But my beautiful brothers, as we have said many times, we learn from our mistakes, and we learn from our active participation in struggle, not from political rhetoric, so we won't cry, but simply fight on; and right on with that. A comrade of mine, Bo, says something that I'd like to leave you with:

"There are two things to remember about revolution, we are going to get our asses kicked, and we are going to win."

"DEATH TO THE FASCIST INSECT THAT PREYS UPON
THE LIFE OF THE PEOPLE."

Fahizah

SCREED ELEVEN

THE HEARST ARREST ORDER

In their search of the "Information Unit" headquarters in Concord, police found sketches of plans to kill and kidnap selected business executives residing in the Bay Area. "Declarations of War" had been drafted against the companies which employed these men, the usual ground being that the companies sold their goods in Rhodesia and South Africa. Among the other records assembled by the Information Unit, but not understood till later, were the name of Steven Weed and the address and telephone number of the deluxe town-house apartment which he shared with Patricia Hearst. Weed, a graduate student in Philosophy, had been Patricia Hearst's mathematics teacher at a private school on the San Francisco Peninsula. They had lived together for two years.

Miss Hearst, as a woman dwelling on a quiet street in a familiar neighborhood, seemed a more simple target to the Berkeley-oriented SLA. She was also a more profitable target. Though she had led an active, even reckless, kind of life, she would register to the public in the familiar double pattern of Child-Victim and Beauty in Distress. From the SLA point of view, her "political" ambiance made her still more attractive. She belonged to the fourth generation of the most distinguished of California dynasties. Her father, Randolph Hearst, had his modest million or so, but also had some access to dozens or scores of millions in the Hearst Foundation and Hearst Corporation. By an even luckier chance, her mother was a member of the Board of Regents which controls operations of the University of California. For many years the Board of Regents had been under violent attack by Berkeley radical and left-wing forces on such matters as government-supported research, "People's Park" development, and student fees. The most recent of the continuing battles against the Regents came from the fact that some University monies were invested in American firms which traded with such no-no nations as South Africa, Portugal, and, unbelievably, Great Britain. The fact that the Hearsts were a newspaper family, with large interests in other media as well, made a grand addition to Patricia Hearst's eligibility as a victim of the SLA.

In the fall of 1973 the Weed-Hearst apartment was looked at by members of Fahizah's SLA Information Unit. On February 2, 1974, a racially mixed SLA team attempted to enter it on a ruse. In the evening of February 4, another racially mixed team one white girl and two Negro men -- got the door opened with a story about an automobile accident, thrust Steven Weed back into the apartment, and chased the screaming Patricia Hearst from room to room. Weed's hands were tied and he was beaten with a wine bottle. A neighbor, Steven Suenaga, rushed in to offer aid, and was clubbed down and left for dead. Weed freed his hands, ran out the back door, and hurried through four back gardens and over three fences before stopping in the safety of another street. After his escape, Patricia Hearst, clothed only in a nightgown, was hustled out of the apartment. A little armada of three cars a Volkswagen bug, an old Chevrolet station wagon, and a stolen convertible had been assembled there by the SLA, and Miss Hearst was thrown bodily into the trunk of the convertible. Some of the six or seven SLA members had begun shooting by then, and the three vehicles disappeared with the revolutionary guns still blazing.

There was a brief news blackout, then some inconclusive statements by police. It seemed understood from the first that it was not a money-oriented kidnapping. Within a few days, the news media had become aware of the marvelous possibilities of the crime as a news story, and crews of reporters and cameramen began to assemble in the grounds of the Hearst estate in the wealthy suburb of Hillsborough, south of San Francisco. On February 7, the SLA sent its "Communique #3," to the left-cum-culture Berkeley radio station KPFA.

Communique #3 is a "warrant order" for the "arrest" of Miss Hearst, and follows the form used in Communique #1, the "warrant order" for the execution of Marcus Foster and Robert Blackburn. Three of its stipulations were to become fixed objectives of the SLA in its long subsequent contest with the Hearst family, the police agencies, and American society in general. These were that "any attempt... by authorities to release the prisoner" would cause her to be executed; that "any attempt... to witness or interfere with any operation" of the SLA will also be met with shootings; and that SLA documents "MUST be published in full" by "all newspapers, and all other forms of the media." Never in history has an outlaw demand so successfully publicized and protected an outlaw organization.

SYMBIONESE LIBERATION ARMY

WESTERN REGIONAL ADULT UNIT

Communique #3
February 4, 1974
Subject: Prisoners of War
Warrant Order: Arrest and protective custody, and if resistance execution
Target: Patricia Campbell Hearst,custody, daughter of Randoph A. Hearst, corporate enemy of the people
Warrant Issued By: The Court of the People

On the afore stated date, combat elements of the United Federated Forces of The Symbionese Liberation Army armed with cyanide loaded weapons served an arrest warrant upon Patricia Campbell Hearst.

It is the order of this court that the subject be arrested by combat units and removed to a protective area of safety and only upon completion of this condition to notify Unit #4 to give communication of this action.

It is the directive of this court that during this action ONLY, no civilian elements be harmed if possible, and that warning shots be given. However, if any citizens attempt to aid the authorities or interfere with the implementation of this order, they shall be executed immediately.

This court hereby notifies the public and directs all combat units in the future to shoot to kill any civilian who attempts to witness or interfere with any operation conducted by the people's forces against the fascist state.

Should any attempt be made by authorities to rescue the prisoner, or to arrest or harm any S.L.A. elements, the prisoner is to be executed.

The prisoner is to be maintained in adequate physical and mental condition, and unharmed as long as these conditions are adhered to. Protective custody shall be composed of combat and medical units, to safeguard both the prisoner and her health.

All communications from this court MUST be published in full, in all newspapers, and all other forms of the media. Failure to do so will endanger the safety of the prisoner.

Further communications will follow.

S.L.A.

DEATH TO THE FASCIST INSECT THAT PREYS UPON
THE LIFE OF THE PEOPLE

SCREED TWELVE

CINQUE'S INDICTMENT

The tape cassette which accompanied the above typed "arrest order" introduced General Field Marshal Cinque to the American public. The name is variously pronounced. As a Spanish name it is Syn-Kay to purists; to Anglos it looks like Sink or Seenkw; its bearer and most other Blacks called it Syn Kew. As the Hearst food program began, it appeared in hero-worshiping graffiti as "Sin Cue." The original Cinque was a Wendi leader, enslaved and en route to America, who led a successful mutiny on the slave-ship L'Amistad in 1839. The legal actions which followed this mutiny were important to the whole nineteenth-century American antislavery movement, and the incident is one of the gems of Black History and Black Identity programs.

The new Cinque was immediately identified in newspapers as Donald David DeFreeze. DeFreeze, an outgoing man of 30, had compiled a record of violent and near-violent crimes in the Middle West and then in California. Most of his activity was merely fiscal, while some, including a bomb incident, was political. During his experience in and out of jails, DeFreeze became interested in Black aspirations. At the beginning of the 1970's he was a leader and lecturer at the Vacaville prison branch of the semi-revolutionary Black Culture Association, or BCA. Two of his associates in that enterprise were Thero Wheeler, 29, a Black prisoner, and Russell Little, one of the white men arrested in Concord and charged with the shooting of Foster and Blackburn. Little, a graduate of the University of Florida, in Philosophy, had been working as a visiting instructor in the BCA program at Vacaville.

Early in 1974, DeFreeze escaped from Soledad Prison and Wheeler from Vacaville: Both immediately joined Little, Remiro, and other pioneer SLA people in Berkeley and Oakland. Shortly after their arrival in the East Bay, DeFreeze put his great personal force behind the idea of a militant SLA as opposed to a slower-moving Symbionese Federation. There was a change in personnel, and many of the former Federation people were so frightened as to leave Berkeley or go into hiding. Dc-Freeze, by then familiar in the East Bay as Cinque, startled the leadership of other radical organizations by offering himself and the SLA as semipro hit men who would eliminate designated enemies on contract. Rejected, he, with his colleagues, seized the opportunity offered by the chaotic Oakland School Board discussions of security in the schools. The attack on Foster and Blackburn further alienated the Bay Area revolutionaries, and at the time of the Hearst kidnapping the SLA stood almost alone.

In his indictment of the Hearsts, which is presented as Screed 12, Cinque nevertheless sticks to the wrongs voiced en masse by the left-radical organizations of Berkeley and environs. His voice on the tape projected as calm and secure, with hints of pleased irony, in accents typical of literate and articulate American Negroes.

To those who would bear the hopes and future of our people, let the voice of their guns express the words of freedom: Greetings to the people, fellow comrades, brothers and sisters.

My name is Cinque, and to my comrades I am known as Cin. I am a Black man and representative of Black people. I hold the rank of general field marshal in the United Federated Forces of the Symbionese Liberation Army.

Today I have received an order from the Symbionese War Council, the Court of the People, to the effect that I am ordered to convey the following message in behalf of the SLA, and to insert a taped word of comfort and verification, that Patricia Campbell Hearst is alive and safe.

The Symbionese Liberation Army is a federated union that maintains political elements of many different liberation struggles, and of many different races. Our unified purpose is to liberate the oppressed people of this nation and to aid other oppressed people around the world in their struggle against fascist imperialism and the robbery of their freedom a n d homeland. Since this is the purpose and goal of the SLA, it is therefore clear to us, as it will be to all oppressed people, that our interest is to serve and defend the people and not ourselves, since the people shall always come first, themselves.

The SLA has arrested the subject [Patricia Hearst] for the crimes that her mother and father have, by their actions, committed against we [sic], the American people, and oppressed people of the world. In understanding this charge, we must first understand who the Hearsts are, and who they serve and represent.

Randolph A. Hearst is the corporate chairman of the fascist media empire of the ultra-right Hearst Corporation, which is one of the largest propaganda institutions of this oppressive military dictatorship of the militarily armed corporate state that we now live under in this nation.

The primary goal of this empire is to save and form [sic] a necessary propaganda and smokescreen to shield the American people from the realities of the corporate dictatorship t h a t Richard Nixon and Gerald Ford represent. This network of propaganda programs and confusion has succeeded in hiding the truth from the people; that truth being that this nation has suffered its first military coup and that the Constitution, which some of us still believe in, has been overthrown.

The fascist Hearst Corporation, composed of, firstly, a national newspaper syndicate which includes the San Francisco Examiner, the Chronicle, and others which jump from California and to as far away as New York and Philadelphia;

Secondly, a magazine monopoly composed of over 13 publications, which include, for example, House Beautiful, Harper's Bazaar, Town and Country and Cosmopolitan;

Thirdly, a TV and radio station empire across the nation, with production and propaganda fields of both national and international use;

Fourth, ownership of vast areas of real estate in the United States and Mexico, forest, grasslands and cattle farms.

All of this is directly connected with Washington and the corporate dictatorship of Richard Nixon and Gerald Ford. That is to say, the Hearst empire is one of the empires of the ruling class and its interests are the rich [sic] and in direct contradiction with the interests of the people. Therefore, they are enemies of the people.

Mrs. Randolph A. Hearst is a member of the University of California Board of Regents and is responsible along with others appointed by Governor Reagan, for the lowering of funds and the investment of our California tax money in corporations which have interests and do gain profits from the robbery, oppression, genocide carried out by fascist and racist governments around the world, and within the United States itself.

The Regents, with the support of Mrs. Hearst, have time and time again been requested by we, the people [sic], to not invest our money in such fascist corporations as General Motors, Westinghouse, Gulf, Standard Oil, Bank of America and others, who have and do serve and gain profit in the oppression, robbery and murder that is committed against Black people of South Africa, where 70,000 Black children a year die from malnutrition; against white people of Ireland, where U.S.-trained British soldiers shoot down in the streets Irish fathers and mothers and U.S. manufactured tear gas suffocates Irish children as their older brothers and sisters rot in British concentration camps; against the freedom of the Philippine people that the United States and Marco's puppet soldiers used U.S. manufactured napalm to attempt to burn away the spirit of freedom from the hearts and souls of the poor and starving [sic].

The U.C. Board of Regents, one of California's largest foreign investors, supports, through its investments, the murder of thousands of Black men and women and children of Mozambique, Angola and Rhodesia, murder designed to destroy the spirit that all humanity longs for.

With all these crimes placed before the Board of Regents and Mrs. Hearst, with all the pleas from the people to stop supporting these corporations and the murders of thousands of men, women and children, the Board and Mrs. Hearst did not raise one voice in protest, or refuse to be part of these crimes committed against these people, and those committed against the American people. For these acts and others, the Court of the People finds the Hearst family accountable for their crimes and hold that they are enemies of the people.

We of the Symbionese Liberation Army hold [that] the Hearst Corporation and the Hearst family and the Board of Regents, as well as the corporate state which they support and aid, are enemies of the people, and that the people have the legal and human right and duty to attack said enemy according to the forms of war taken by the oppressed people against any enemy or murderer and oppressor to regain their freedom and liberty and to give love to their children and people.

It is therefore the directive of this Court that before any forms of negotiations for the release of the subject prisoner be initiated, that an action of good faith be shown on the part of the Hearst family to allow the court and the oppressed people of this world and this nation to ascertain as to the real interests and cooperative attitude of the Hearst family and in so doing, show some form of repentance for the murder and suffering they have aided and profited from; and this good faith gesture is to be in the form of a token gesture to the oppressed people that aid [sic?] the corporate state in robbing and removing their rights to freedom and liberty.

This gesture is to be in the form of food to the needy and unemployed, and to which [sic] the following instructions are to be followed to the letter.

In closing, and speaking personally for myself, and as a father of two children, I wish to say to Mr. Hearst and Mrs. Hearst that I, as also the persons under my command for the authority of the Court of the People, are not savage killers and madmen, and we do hold a high moral value to life [sic]. We value life very deeply, and with all the spirit that we, as human beings, can bring forth in our hearts.

Speaking as a father, I am quite willing to lose both my children, if by that action I could save thousands of white, black, yellow and red children from a life of suffering, exploitation and murder. And I am therefore quite willing to carry out the execution of your daughter to save the life of starving men, women and children of every race; and I, along with the loyal men and women of many races who love the people, quite willingly give our lives to free the people at any cost.

And if, as you and others might so easily believe, that we will lose, let it be known that even in death we will win, for the very ashes of this fascist nation will mark our very grave [sic].

SCREED THIRTEEN

PATRICIA HEARST'S FIRST TAPE

Patricia Hearst's voice on the first tape was broadcast throughout the nation only a few hours after its being received at Station KPFA on February 12. Her voice was thin and strained, and it was immediately conjectured that she spoke under the influence of medical sedation or street drugs. Her discourse was also chopped into short sections by starting and stopping of the tape recorder.

The matter on the tape is important as expressing continuing concerns of the SLA. Miss Hearst's carefully schooled discourse disavows identity of the SLA with other groups (especially the August Seventh), insists on the character of the SLA as a legitimate army engaged in warfare, and hints at a numerous as well as carefully organized system of SLA units. Her great worry, or that of her abductors, came from the possibility that the police would try to take the secret prison by storm. From the very beginning, many people believed that the FBI and local police knew where she was being held, as well as the names of all her abductors, and the SLA seems to have believed this also. The "house in Oakland" to which she refers was raided by Oakland police after receipt of a distress call.

Patricia Hearst's reference to the captivity of Remiro and Little as analogous to her own captivity begins the long period of confusion about what the SLA expected by way of prisoner-privilege and prisoner exchange. Remiro and Little were in San Quentin for security reasons, to protect them from possible attack by other prisoners in county jails. The fact that they were lodged in a famous state prison without having been tried for any crime was good propaganda, and was picked up in later screeds.

Mom, Dad,

I'm OK. I had a few scrapes and stuff, but they washed them up and they're getting OK. And I caught a cold, but they are giving me pills for it and stuff. I am not being starved or beaten or unnecessarily frightened. I have heard some press reports, and so I know that Steve and all the neighbors are OK and that no one was really hurt.

And I also know that the SLA members here are very upset about press distortions of what's been happening. They have nothing to do with the August 7th movement. They have not been shooting down helicopters or shooting down innocent people in the streets.

I'm kept blindfolded usually so that I can't identify anyone. My hands are often tied, but generally they're not. I'm not gagged or anything, and I'm comfortable. And I think you can tell that I'm not really terrified or anything and that I'm okay.

I was very upset though to hear about police rushing in on that house in Oakland, and I was really glad that I wasn't there. And I would appreciate it if everyone would just calm down and try not to find me and not be making identifications, because they're not only endangering me but they're endangering themselves.

I am with a combat unit that's armed with automatic weapons and there's also a medical team here and there's no way that I will be released until they let me go, so it won't do any good for somebody to come in here and try to get me out by force.

These people aren't just a bunch of nuts. They've been really honest with me but they're perfectly willing to die for what they are doing. And I want to get out of here but the only way I'm going is if we do it their way. And I just hope that you'll do what they say, Dad, and just do it quickly.

I've been stopping and starting this tape myself, so that I can collect my thoughts. That's why there are so many stops in it.

I'm not being forced to say any of this. I think it's really important that you take their requests very seriously about not arresting any other SLA members and about following their good faith request to the letter. I just want to get out of here and see everyone again and be back with Steve.

The SLA is very interested in seeing how you're taking this, Dad, and they want to make sure that you are really serious and listening to what they're saying. And they t h i n k that you've been t a k i n g this whole thing a lot more seriously than the police and the FBI and other federal people have been taking it.

It seems to be getting to the point where they're not worried about you so much as they're worrying about other people. Or at least I am. It's really up to you to make sure that these people don't jeopardize my life by charging in and doing stupid things, and I hope you will make sure that they don't do anything else like that Oakland house business.

The SLA people really have been honest with me and I really, I mean I feel pretty sure, that I'm going to get out of here if everything goes the way they want it to. And I think you should feel that way too and try not to worry so much. I mean I know it's hard but I heard that Mom was really upset and that everybody was at home. I hope that this puts you a little bit at ease so that you know that I really am all right. I just hope that I can get back to everybody really soon.

The SLA has ideological ties with the IRA, the people's struggle in the Philippines and the Socialist people in Puerto Rico in their struggle for independence, and they consider themselves to be soldiers who are fighting and aiding these people.

I am a prisoner of war and so are the two men in San Quentin. I am being treated in accordance with the Geneva Convention, one of the conditions being that I am not being tried for crimes which I'm not responsible for.

I am here because I am a member of a ruling class family, and I think you can begin to see the analogy. The people, the two men in San Quentin, are being held and are going to be tried simply because of the SLA and not because they've done anything. Witnesses to the shooting of Foster saw black men. And two white men have been arrested for this.

You're being told this so that you'll understand why I was kidnapped, and so that you'll understand that whatever happens to the two prisoners is going to happen to me. You have to understand that I am held to be innocent the same way the two men in San Quentin are innocent, [and] that they are simply members of the group, and had not done anything themselves to warrant their arrest. They apparently were part of an intelligence unit and have never executed anyone themselves.

The SLA has declared war against the government and it's important that you understand that they know what they're doing and [that] they understand what their actions mean. And that you realize that this is not considered by them to be just a simple kidnapping, and that you don't treat it that way and say "Oh, I don't know why she was taken".

I'm telling you now why this happened so that you will know and so that you'll have something to use, some knowledge to try to get me out of here. If you can get the food thing organized before the 19th, then that's OK, and it would just speed up my release.

Today is Friday the eighth and in Kuwait the commandos negotiated the release of their hostages and they left the country.

Bye.

SCREED FOURTEEN

THE SIDEMAN'S SUMMARY

After Patricia Hearst's message, a summary or situation report was given. The voice was immediately identified as that of Thero Wheeler, who had worked in Cinque's Black Culture program at Vacaville, and escaped from that prison at the time Cinque escaped from Soledad. The voice on the tape is less experienced than that of Cinque. Wheeler, if it was he, spoke from a script, and sometimes slipped away from it and tangled the syntax. Soon after, he fled the SLA.

Mr. Hearst:

As your daughter has said, she is being held under the international codes of war. And, as she is not going to be harmed in any manner unless any [sic] attempt is made to release her by force, she is being properly treated, properly fed, and she has an exercise area, fresh air, and so forth. And she is not being harmed in any fashion.

And this is also related to our captured soldiers that are being held in San Quentin. And we hope that they will receive the same treatment, according to the international codes of war.

We understand from the national reports and so forth that the police authorities and others are attempting to place the responsibility upon us, in saving the life of your daughter [sic] and to distort and mislead the realities of the matter [sic].

However, we wish to express to you, and to the authorities, and to the public, that whatever happens to your daughter will be totally your responsibility, and the responsibility of the authorities which you represent. Her life will be maintained in the fashion, that is, according to, the terms of war. And if they, or yourself, violate these, her life and her blood, if that, will be upon your hands only.

In regards to communications. For security reasons, and because of where we are at [sic], there is, not possible [sic], for us to maintain a continuous flow of communications with you. So don't expect phone calls, communications, three or four times a week. Because they won't come.

When the stated good faith gesture is conducted [sic], and we have means to ascertain as to if they are [sic], we will begin negotiations for the release of your daughter. Until then, you can be sure, and have our word, whatever that may be to you, that we will carry out our word to the letter. And we mean exactly what we say.

DEATH TO THE FASCIST INSECTS THAT PREYS
UPON THE LIFE OF THE PEOPLE.

SCREED FIFTEEN

GOOD FAITH FOOD

The idea of spreading food among the poor by means of extortion has had its major successes in South America, where poverty truly means hunger and may even mean starvation. Its SLA importation to the United States, where poverty has different meanings, was described by the columnist Max Lerner as "a kind of morality play in which the United States is depicted as starving its needy; and the revolutionaries as daring knights who perform deeds of great risk and valor to feed them" Lerner correctly added that the media, with its continual interest in the absurd and the poignant, and its lack of interest in probabilities and truth, "played the game of the terrorists".

In the demand for free food, the SLA miscalculated both the identity of "the poor" and the fortune of Randolph Hearst. Their list of recipient groups engrossed millions of Californians who were prosperous, and tens of thousands who classed as rich. Nothing about Social Security or military disability, for example, connotes any kind of poverty. It was immediately headlined all over California that the Hearst ransom, if paid out in full, would amount to a half-billion dollars. This original confusion of thinking was to lead to many other well-reported muddles before the Hearst free food program was finished.

Had possible demands been made, and strictly carried out, the position would have remained the same. All three of the original speakers (Screeds 12, 13, 14) had stipulated that the free food would not be a ransom but a "good-faith gesture", meant to test "the real interest and cooperative attitude of the Hearst family". Through it the Hearsts would begin to show their "repentance for the murder and suffering they have aided and profited from". The question of Miss Hearst's fate would remain open. The Berkeley girls promised nothing.

Most of the organizations listed in Screed 15 as overseers or critics of the free food program are Black or Black-dominated. All are tax-exempt and some are tax-supported. Except for the San Francisco Chinatown location, and for Santa Rosa (Fahizah's home town), the specified locations are also Black in the main. The continuing desire of the SLA for media coverage gives rise to all articles of Section B.

(Section) A---

We have heard it said that Mr. Hearst wants to save his daughter, [but] we want to save all the children and people. In an effort to answer some of the basic needs of the people, we are asking for a symbolic gesture of good faith from this representative of the corporate state.

Each person with one of the following cards is to be given $70.00 worth of meats, vegetables, and dairy products: All people with welfare cards, social security pension cards, food stamp cards, disabled veteran cards, medical cards, parole or probation papers, and jail or bail release slips. So that all those with such cards have time, and will not be forced to stand waiting in long lines, the time for the distribution of this food must extend over a four week period, beginning February 19th. On each Tuesday, Thursday, and Saturday for four successive weeks, each person with one of the listed cards can go to publicized stores and pick up their food.

1. The stores where people can go are to be clearly designated and publicized in each of the communities listed below, and they are to be within easy access to the people of those communities. There must be at least S stores as distribution points within each community; these distribution points should be major stores within the community, we suggest such stores as Safeway and Mayfair.

2. The meat, vegetables, and dairy products must be of top quality, and in ample supply during all store hours.

3. TO THE PEOPLE: If you are not receiving your food, all you have to do is voice your discontent in the streets, at bus stops, movie theaters, etc. and we will hear about it. Also anyone facing any interference from the police state in the way of harassment should voice their discontent. The people's army calls upon community groups such as Nirobi [ie, Nairobi] College in East Palo Alto, Glide Memorial Church in San Francisco, and The Black Teachers Caucus, the National Welfare Rights Organization, United Farm Workers, AIM, Third World Womens Alliance, United Prisoner's Union, as well as representatives from people's news services such as Getting Together, Kalayan, Triple Jeopardy, Black Panther Party, The Anvil, and others to act as observers and coordinators to see to it that the aged and disabled receive their food and ways to transport it and shop for it, AND to see to it that NO police-state agents, in or out of uniform, are allowed to be in the areas of food distribution, or photograph or harass the people.

4. Stores in each of the following cities or communities are to serve as distribution points:

San Francisco (Mission District, Chinatown, Hunters Point, The Fillmore)
Oakland (East and west)
Delano
Richmond

Santa Rosa
East Palo Alto
Los Angeles (Watts Compton, East Los Angeles)

(Section) B--

1. The document showing the emblem and meaning of the seven-headed cobra that is in the possession of police state authorities shall be placed in newspapers and other forms of the media in its exact form, not omitting any area.

2. The document that is enclosed regarding the declaration of war and the goals of The S.L.A. shall also be placed in its total form in newspapers and other forms of the media.

3. A copy of all these stated documents, along with a full copy of the tape enclosed recorded by myself [ie, Cinque?] and Pat Hearst is to be distributed to the media for publication.

4. The news media is warned that all attempts to mislead the public concerning the intentions of The S.L.A., or to confuse the public by withholding or omitting sections of the tape or S.L.A. documents, jeopardizes the prisoner.

IF THIS GESTURE OF GOOD FAITH IS NOT MET, THEN WE WILL ASSUME THAT THERE IS NO BASIS FOR NEGOTIATIONS, AND WE WILL NO LONGER TAKE, AND MAINTAIN IN GOOD HEALTH AND SPIRITS, PRISONERS OF WAR.

S.L.A.

SCREED SIXTEEN

PATRICIA HEARST CONCILIATES

From its first publication, the half-billion dollar free-food demand received saturation reportage. There was considerable jostling among organizations named as proctors or overseers, each taking its own attitude and earning its own reportage. A star system gradually developed, with one leader and then another occupying the front pages and the television screens.

Great early attention was given to the two American Indian Movement (AIM) leaders, Russell Means and Dennis Banks, who had become world news during their occupation of Wounded Knee, South Dakota, a year earlier. Now under indictment for theft, arson, and other crimes, and rejected as "hoodlums" by their parent tribe the Oglala Sioux, they came to San Francisco and were heavily interviewed and photographed. A by-product of their visit was the official opposing statement of nineteen legitimate Indian groups in the Bay Area. Through their spokesmen and spokeswomen, these groups attacked the SLA and declined all interest in the food program.

Following Means and Banks into the limelight was Rev. Cecil Williams, the hippie-style semi-revolutionary pastor of the Black-oriented Glide Memorial Church in San Francisco. Williams, in several television interviews, had expressed sympathy with the objectives of the SLA and refused to condemn their tactics. To him, consequently, the SLA sent its next tape. Following his receipt of it, he went to Hillsborough and was photographed with the Hearsts and others, and interviewed in saturation style. His preeminence among the food-plan notables lasted over a week.

Patricia Hearst's voice on the new tape was much stronger and more confident. She spoke ad lib, with the verbal hesitations and confusions fashionable to her generation, but from carefully worded notes. In addition to the expected references to her danger, to her war-prisoner status, and to her match-off with Remiro and Little, she carefully outlined the SLA's philosophical justification for deeds of violence, extortion, and media-grabbing. Her "Mr. Bates" is the FBI spokesman and chief agent on the case.

Miss Hearst's SLA prompters went on with their efforts to direct public opinion. Her earnest insistence that the SLA is "not a racial thing" reflects the troublesome fact that the food operation was under increasing denunciation from non-Black groups. By this time almost every racial, radical, or revolutionary fragment had officially denounced the SLA. Many Black organizations, including groups led by Coretta Scott King and Angela Davis, had also drawn back, but without affecting the increasingly Black tone of the SLA image.

Voice of Patricia Hearst

Dad, Mom,

I am making this tape to let you know that I'm still OK and to explain a few things, I hope.

First, about the good faith gesture. There was some misunderstanding about that, and you should do what you can and they understand that you want to meet their demands and that [pause] they have every intention that you should be able to meet their demands.

They were not trying to present an unreasonable request. It was never intended that you feed the whole state. So whatever you come up with is basically OK. And just do it as fast as you can, and everything will be fine.

But the SLA is really mad about certain attempts to make the feeding of food [sic] be the receiving of goods that were gotten by extortion. And they don't want people to be harassed by the police or by anybody else, and I hope you can do something about that. And if you can't, well, I mean, they'll do something about it.

So [pause] you shouldn't worry about that too much.

Also, I would like to emphasize that I am alive and that I am well, and that in spite what certain tape experts seem to think. I mean I'm fine. It's really depressing to hear people talk about me like I'm dead. I can't explain what it's like.

What it does, also, is that it [pause] begins to convince other people that maybe I am dead. If everybody is convinced that I am dead, well, then it gives the FBI an excuse to come in here and try to pull me out. I'm sure that Mr. Bates understands that if the FBI has to come in and get me out by force, that they [ie, SLA?] won't have time to decide who not to kill. They'll just have to kill everyone. I don't particularly want to die that way. I hope you will realize that everything is OK and that they'll just have to back off for a while. There will be plenty of time for investigating later.

I am basically an example and a symbolic warning, not only to you but to everyone, that there are people who are not going to accept your support of other governments and that, faced with suppression and murder of the people [pause]. And this is a warning to everybody.

It is also to show what can be done. When it is necessary, the people can be fed, and to show that. It is too bad that it has to happen this way, to make people see that there are people who need food. Now maybe something can be done about that, so that things like this won't have to happen again. [pause]

Also, the SLA is very annoyed about attempts by the press and by authorities to turn this into a racial issue. It's not. This is a political issue and this is a political action that they've taken. Anyone who really reads the stated objectives of the SLA can see very clearly that this is not a racial thing. So I hope there won't be any more confusion about that. [pause]

I turned over my notes here, so [pause].

I am being held as a prisoner of war and not as anything else, and I am being held in accordance with international codes of war. And so you should not listen or believe what anybody else says about the way I'm being treated. This is the way I'm being treated. I am not left alone and I am not just shoved off, I mean. I am fine; I am not being starved, and I am not being beaten or tortured. Really.

Since I am an example, it's really important that everyone understand that I am an example and a warning. And because of this, it is very important to the SLA that I return safely. So people should stop acting like I'm dead. Mom should get out of her black dress. That doesn't help at all.

I wish you'd try to understand the position I'm in. I am right in the middle, and I have to depend upon what all kinds of other people are going to do. And it's really hard for me to hear about reports of, you know, and [pause]. I hope you understand and try to do something.

I know that a lot of people have written and everyone is concerned about me and my safety, and about what you are going through. I want them all to know that I'm OK. And it [blurred sound, "it's important?"] for them to understand that I will be OK as long as the SLA demands are met, and as long as the two prisoners in San Quentin are OK.

And as long as the FBI doesn't come in here. That is my biggest worry. I think I can get out of here alive as long as they don't come bursting in.

And I really think you should understand that the SLA does have an interest in my return. And try not to worry so much. And just do what you can. I mean, I know you're doing everything. Take care of Steve. And hurry. Bye.

On Wednesday, Solzhenitsyn was exiled to West Germany.

Voice of Male Captor

This is General Field Marshal Cin speaking. (Donald DeFreeze)

We wish to clarify what your daughter has said about our request for a good-faith gesture on your part.

The people are awaiting your gesture. You may rest assured that we are quite able to assess the extent of your sincerity in this matter and we will accept a sincere effort on your part.

We are quite able to be aware of the extent of your capabilities, as we are also aware of the needs of the people.

Death to the fascist insect that preys upon the life of the people.

SCREED SEVENTEEN

A TAPE OF REVISION AND RAGE

By the middle of February it had become the habit of Randolph A. Hearst to come out of his mansion in Hillsborough daily for an exchange with the still-growing army of reporters and cameramen assembled on his lawn. On February 18, he began the interview by reading a statement bearing his conciliatory counter-offer to the SLA.

In this statement, Hearst said that he had completed arrangements to deliver two million dollars to a "tax-exempt charitable organization" which would "distribute food to the poor and needy". Half a million of this, "a substantial part of my personal assets", would come out of his own pocket. The remainder would come from the William Randolph Hearst Foundation, an independently managed public-service institution. Since Remiro and Little had some still-obscure but certainly important part in the transaction, he added that he had directed the prominent lawyer, William Coblentz, to see that they "get a fair trial and receive due process in all phases of the proceedings".

Coblentz subsequently visited the pair in San Quentin and reported that they were well treated and well represented by council. It was the food part of the statement that was to rankle the SLA, and, for one month, to control the media. An offer to administer the food program had been made by A. Ludlow Kramer, an energetic politician from the State of Washington. Kramer had successfully administered a free food program in Seattle, catering especially to people who had become unemployed by the reduction of staff in the local Boeing plant.

There was to be an independent foundation with its own name, "People in Need", or PIN. PIN was to use the Hearst money as mere seed-money, meanwhile collecting many millions in cash, food, and services from well-meaning people and institutions all over America. It was to be "ongoing" or even "permanent", and in the first year of its life it would "feed", an uncertain term, "100,000 people per month". Kramer's Seattle plan, gotten up in years of great food surpluses, and designed for a stable and responsible working-class clientele, had been meant to help families who were also helping themselves. It was a "supplemental" program, and Kramer early introduced the name "supplemental" to the Hearst program as well.

Screed 17, the first attack on the plan, was read onto tape by Field Marshal Cinque on February 19, one day after Hearst's offer of two millions. It divides into five clear parts, all supposedly derived from a "hearing" in the SLA Court of the People. This time Cinque spoke with anger, even with rage. A one-line addendum by Miss Hearst established the date and made a sinister suggestion about her own future. Once more the tape was delivered by agency of Rev. Cecil Williams. Williams and his associates picked it up in the San Francisco Public Library, listened to it in their headquarters at Glide Church, and then "called Randy Hearst and reported to him".

Four of the five parts of the tape have the function of explaining and justifying Part 3, the action part at the center. In Part 1 Cinque, speaking for the Court, reviews his former communication about money, food, and good faith. In Part 2 he lists the enormous investments and holdings attributed to the Hearsts, and the imputedly criminal sources of this wealth. In Part 4, after the carefully specified demands in Part 3, the central part, he returns to the theories of cooperation and alliance between revolutionary and "people's" organizations which had been the burden of early SLA screeds. His intense concern about relations between the SLA and other radical, revolutionary, and social-fraction groups probably registers the SLA's sense of growing isolation. In the final movement, Part 5, departing from his formerly rational tones, Cinque indulges in a passionate diatribe, almost an ode, in which hate, rage, and vengefulness are openly exposed.

In the middle part, here named Part 3, Cinque and his SLA colleagues had meanwhile tacitly acknowledged some errors. The new screed asked for less. The open-ended first demand was reduced to a demand for six million dollars. The idea of giving each recipient a $70 bundle was abandoned; now each would get seventy dollars during the course of one month. The specification that no identification need be shown by recipients reflects the outraged rejection of all such benefits by organizations of the card-holders mentioned in the first demand. And the geographical scope of the program was reduced, so that all distribution would be in the Bay Area.

But new conditions were added, too. The specification that all food be "of good quality", and that no "surplus storage goods or government commodities" be distributed, effectively cut the heart out of Kramer's plans for an "ongoing" system of "supplemental" rations. Finally, the appointment of the Western Addition Project Area Committee, or WAPAC, as the chief overseer among the overseeing "coalition of the people's community organizations" provided a new star in the constellation that had formed around the food program. WAPAC was a government-supported agency operating through political means to better the lives of "the poor" in a predominantly Black neighborhood of San Francisco. It had earned its place at the head of the Coalition by virtue of some news conferences in which its leadership expressed sympathy for the SLA people. Its principal leader, Arnold Townsend, immediately replaced Rev. Cecil Williams as the media star of the food operation, and soon rivaled Kramer as its theoretician and director.

The Voice of Marshal Cinque

To those who bear the hopes and faith of our people, the voice of the guns expresses the words of freedom.

Greetings to the people, comrades, sisters and brothers. This is General Field Marshal Cinque speaking.

[I]

The Symbionese War Council has just finished hearing tapes and hearing some of the news reports and statements made by the Hearst Family concerning the arrest of Patricia Campbell Hearst.

In the Court's second tape by Patricia, [ie, Screed 16] it was said that any

good faith gesture on the part of the Hearst empire would be "basically OK."
We, however, understand that Patricia wants to come home as soon as possible, and that this statement was clearly misinterpreted as meaning that an
untrue gesture of good faith and regret would be accepted by the people.
This is not the case and, therefore, at the end of that tape stated by Patricia, I
myself, by the direction of the court, stated the feeling of the court and thereby clarifying the request of the people.

That statement reads as follows:

We wish to clarify what your daughter has said about our request by a good
faith gesture on your part. The people are awaiting your gesture. You may rest
assured that we are quite able to assess the extent of your sincerity in this matter. And we will accept a sincere effort on your part.

We are quite able and aware of the extent of your capabilities, as we are also
aware of the needs of the people.

The Hearst empire has attempted to mislead the people and to deceive them
by claiming to put forth a good faith gesture of $2 million. This amount is
not at all a good faith gesture but rather is an act of throwing a few crumbs to
the people, forcing them to fight over it [sic] amongst themselves.

We have had a court hearing concerning both the actions of the enemy
Hearst family and the Hearst empire as a whole, and the media, and the combined responsible gesture of good faith.

We have chosen first to expose a sampling of the extent of the Hearst empire, which includes the Hearst Foundation, the Hearst Corporation empire,
and Mr. and Mrs. Hearst's personal assets. The assets of the Hearsts' wealth
include the following:

1. A silver mine and thousands of acres of land in Mexico, acreage in Hawaii,
and 70,000 acres of timberland in Northern California valued at millions of
dollars. A cattle ranch near San Luis Obispo, orange groves in Florida, a duck
club and rice paddies outside of Marysville, Calif. Small land holdings and
homes in Hillsborough, New York and San Diego. Each valued at well over
one-half million dollars.

2. Personal stocks. Large interests in IBM, Beatrice Foods, Exxon, the Sugar

Bowl Corps., and Safeway stores, United Airlines, and Hughes Airways. And huge holdings in drug companies, ore industries, paper companies, lumber companies and cattle ranches.

3. Miscellaneous personal items. A collection of antique paintings, Chinese screens and Greek vases. Twenty-four vases each valued at $10,000 each. A collection of Oriental rugs given to him by his personal friend, the Shah of Iran. The family has also received numerous gifts over the years from other long-time personal friends such as Howard Hughes.

The Hearst Foundation is a front for the Hearst fortune. The foundation serves as a tax loophole for that fortune. The foundation donates $3 million a year to established charities to maintain its status as a foundation. The $1.5 million proposed to be coming from the foundation is nothing more than half of what that foundation is legally required to donate annually in order to maintain its foundation status.

The assets of the Hearst Corp have been stated many times However, I will restate them again as some specific factors. As we all know, the Hearst Corp. is composed of a chain of magazines and newspapers. However, I wish to point out two specific ones as examples *Cosmopolitan* magazine reaps profits of $7 millions to $8 millions per year. Another is *House Beautiful*, which reaps profits of $3 million to $4 million a year. The Hearst Corp. is also composed of, as mentioned before, a chain of TV stations and feature film industries and also ownership of lumber companies and partnership in large stock holdings in General Motors, as well as land holdings in each of the cities where the newspaper chains operate: for example, ownership of one square block in New York City, with the land alone valued in hundreds of millions of dollars, as well as land and buildings in England and Australia and Europe.

[II]

In total, the Hearst empire along with Mr and Mrs Hearst's personal wealth does in fact go into the hundreds and hundreds of millions.

Even if Mr. Hearst was to give all that to the people, with personal friends such as the Shah of Iran and Howard Hughes he would suffer no losses.

However, even if Mr. Hearst were to give all of that to the people, he could never pay the people back for the past losses of their children and freedom, nor for the current suffering they are now under.

We also wish to point out that when necessary the enemy cannot adjust its losses to correspond to its interest at any given time.

It is in the direct interest of Mr. Hearst to comply with the demand for food. Not because he finds it necessary to feed the people but rather because he must secure and protect one of his possessions, his daughter, Patricia. Thus, he finds a way to change the proposal in unacceptable ways [or laws] which allow him to distribute charitable rather than ransom goods.

In the same vein with the stated enemy, corporations wish to aid such countries such as South Africa, the Philippines, South Vietnam, or Ireland in securing brutal dictatorships which rob and murder the people. No existing laws are honored and no one responsible goes to prison for the rest of their lives. This is typified in the Watergate scheme and the U.S. deliberate violation of the United Nations sanctioned international embargo of Rhodesian goods.

On the other hand, any time the interests of the people are at hand there is an enemy law to counteract those interests, and of course the people are forced to abide by them. In understanding this, we come to understand why the U.S. has more prisons, and the largest numbers of laws to control the people, that has ever been recorded in the history of humans on this earth. These laws are created to imprison the people, and by that protect the rich from the poor.

[III]

The plan proposed by Mr. Hearst is not at all acceptable as a gesture of good faith in its present form. It shall be acceptable only in so far as it totally meets the specifications as listed in the following:

1. That an additional $4 million be added to the $2 million already allotted, making a total of $6 million to be used for the purchase of food. We recognize that at wholesale prices available to Mr. Hearst in his designated "Peoples In Need" charity organization, he will be able to feed all who come to receive food. We specify wholesale prices here because we did not intend for Safeway or any other supermarket to make a profit from feeding the poor. Nor do we intend for this to be another program which subsidizes the food industry.

2. That this total $6 million figure be disbursed to the cities of San Francisco, Oakland, and East Palo Alto. That an adequate number of distribution centers be made available to various communities in these cities. San Francisco: Mission District; Chinatown, Hunters Point, the Western Addition, Oakland: East and West. Palo Alto: East Palo Alto.

3. That all foods distributed be of top quality. And that all canned goods and dry foods be matched with their equal amounts of top quality fresh meats, dairy products and produce. And that no attempt be made to distribute garbage, or clothes, or surplus storage foods or government commodities to the people.

4. That $70 be given over a one-month period to each family coming to receive food. That is, by the end of one month's time, a total of $70 of food will have been given to each family. This is to be done during the first month of operation of the program. If this means problems of the storage of food at the distribution center, there is the necessity to have an expansion of the number of centers as well as the number of days and hours that the centers are open. It has always been the intention of the SLA and the Court of the People that a substantial number of families in at least several communities be able to receive their amount of food during this one-month period that would meet some of their needs, in addition to assuring that the people get something more than another extended program which could be abandoned by the Hearsts at any time without the people having ever really received anything. For we have no basis on which to formulate a trust than [sic] an enemy of the people could surely extend a gesture for one year or for any on-going process. Further it is the decision of this Court that $6 per month for a year is in no way [as] beneficial as $70 a month.

5. No names shall be taken or any other form of identification or any addresses of any people who come to receive food. Any people who come to receive food shall get it. There shall be absolutely no questionnaires, forms, or any other type of program processing, which people coming to get food should have to go through. And no form of identification or verification of need other than a simple verbal request for food shall be required.

6. That members of the coalition of the peoples' community organizers and groups be made up of not only the six example organizations named, but any peoples' organizations who wish to participate with the San Francisco Western Addition Project Area Committee known as WAPAC acting as chairman

if they so desire. And that this coalition act solely in the capacity as observers and coordinators, and not negotiators between the SLA combat forces and Mr. Hearst, to see to it that the aged and disabled receive their food, and ways to transport it and shop for it. And to see to it that no police agents in or out of uniform are allowed to be in the areas of food distribution, or photograph or harass the people. And that is to be the leadership of the coalition who should see to it that the distribution centers are run in the true spirit of revolutionary cooperatives, with no bureaucratic overseers or hirelings in the peoples' distribution centers.

7. That we hereby request that the San Francisco Western Addition Project Areas Committee known as WAPAC is hereby designated (if they accept this request) as chairman of the coalition, and has full veto power in the actions and activities of the coalition. We request this and ask this because of that organization's example of showing the people that they serve only the interest of the people, and that they desire to feed the people by any means necessary, and that they did not compromise the needs of the people for the sake of their leadership positions or for the sake of their organization. Rather, without being requested, they stepped forward to show themselves to be in interest of the people.

8. That this tape and a transcript be published and printed in full, omitting nothing, in all forms of the media.

9. That the total amount of $6 million be allotted to your designated "Peoples in Need" or charity organizations within 24 hours of receipt of this order and that the food be available to the people within one week of receipt of this order.

Should this order be rejected, all further communications shall be suspended and the prisoner will be maintained according to the terms of the international codes of war concerning prisoners of war and will be maintained in that status until such time as the status of our captive soldiers is changed. Should any attempt be made to rescue the subject prisoner or to injure or capture our captive soldiers, the subject is to be executed immediately.

10. Once we see compliance with these specifications and the program well under way, then, as we have previously stated, we will begin negotiations for the release of your daughter. The Court of the People also wishes to state that we understand the position of different political organizations requested by

the court to oversee distribution of food. We understand that refusal to participate is partially due to the inherent dangers based upon leadership or the organization as a whole as affiliation with the SLA is stated.

We also feel that it is partially due to lack of understanding of the common enemy as well as a desire to accept reform and revisionism, which are pacifiers against true change in revolution. But for those who do see the necessity to participate in this action and who do recognize the needs of the people, we again state that we are asking only that you function as coordinators and observers for the distribution of food, and that you are not to serve as liaisons, spokesmans, or negotiators for the SLA unless clearly defined as such by writing or by tape.

[IV]

In our previous communiques, we called upon all community groups, including certain specific ones, to act as observers and coordinators. There are basically three stances that these groups can show to the people:

1. Some stand with the people and actively accept the responsibility of working and fighting for the people.

2. Others don't stand at all.

3. Some stand and then slide up next to the enemy's power, serves with the individual organizations instead of the people.

Through this we grow to understand that where an organization or a group of organizations is presented to the enemy as in this case, the enemy will attempt to only negotiate with the political leadership that is most willing to compromise the need and interest of the people and who have the most willingness to call for reform rather than freedom for all people.

This is not to condemn these organizations or their leadership but rather to suggest the people work with these groups and organizations, and educate them and their leaders to serve the interest of the people at all cost and at all times.

We also wish to express to the people how important it is to recognize the meaning of the enemy strategy. We must recognize that enemy propaganda and psychological warfare will be used throughout the struggle for freedom. We must combat enemy attempts to demoralize us, for in the face of failure to achieve military solutions against the people's army, the enemy has to then step up its efforts in the propaganda war.

Their aim is to (1) prevent a liberation movement to get under way by destroying it at its source. That is, by undermining the will to fight. And (2) where revolutionary warfare has actually begun, to conquer it by political means. That is to say by granting just sufficient political economic and social reform for the moment, to encourage all but the so called extremists to abandon the struggle and then kill off the leadership of the people as in the period of King and Malcolm, and then reinstate as a deity oppression and murder of the then defenseless people.

In stating these facts we wish to say that the collective leadership of the SLA would not under any circumstances or under any terms compromise our position or that of the peoples' freedom. And no one should attempt to speak for us or assume that they, by word or action, can compromise any request made on behalf of the people by the SLA.

At this time we wish to state that the organizations who [sic] wish to take part in feeding the people should also cry out for the thousands of children of all colors who have been murdered and starved by the enemy state. They should cry out for the millions of children of all races who are starving and dying now, and not just cry out for the safety of only one human being, who just happens to be the daughter of the enemy of the people.

Fight and cry out in defense of millions and save the children. And by this action you will save also the life of one who has never seen the robbed, or knew [sic] that the riches of her life were the spoils of a robber and a murderer.

[V]

It is in the judgment of this Court that the Hearst family and the Hearst Corp. seems to be more foolishly concerned with the identities of supposed SLA elements rather than with the admission to the people of the crimes committed against the people by the Hearst empire. That by acts of good faith, in [tape hiatus] showing to the people, not to the SLA, the Hearst empire should demonstrate a change of interest, regret for his crimes against the people and a firm decision that they will no longer be a party to such actions in the future.

They should also demonstrate that they are not only concerned with freeing and making a better life for Patricia, but also [with] freeing and making a better life for all of the people.

However, they have seemingly said by their actions that they know me, and therefore do not have to repent for their crimes.

However, to this I would say yes. You do, indeed, know me. You have always known me. I'm that nigger you have hunted and feared night and day. I'm that nigger you have killed hundreds of my people in a vain hope of finding. I'm that nigger that is no longer just hunted, robbed and murdered. I'm the nigger that hunts you now.

Yes, you know me You know me, I'm the wetback You know me, I'm the gook, the broad, the servant, the spic.

Yes indeed, you know us all, and we know you, the oppressor, murderer and robber. And you have hunted and robbed and exploited us all. Now we are the hunters that will give you no rest. And we will not compromise the freedom of our children.

Death to the Fascist insect that preys upon the life of the people.

The Voice of Patricia Hearst

Today is the 19th of February and yesterday the Shah of Iran had two people executed at dawn.

SCREED EIGHTEEN

TELL IT, TELL IT, GET IT RIGHT

After sending out their angry Screed 17, the Symbionese observed two weeks of silence. During this period the attention of the press and electronic media shifted away from the organization itself and focused on the Hearst food giveaway. In the early days of March, Bay Area news people went from the Symbionese to other newsworthy events especially towards new setbacks to President Nixon in his Watergate troubles, towards new developments in the gasoline crisis, and towards a crippling strike by municipal workers and teachers in San Francisco. The silence of the Symbionese contributed to the burial of their own plans behind these emerging new events.

Predestined to failure by its rationale and by the wrong ideas of its leaders, the Hearst food program produced news-comedy rather than the news-portentousness planned for it. In early days of the free food distribution, riots occurred in Oakland and San Francisco. In several locations, Black recipients looted the Hearst supplies, broke into adjacent stores, and looted liquor and tobacco from neighboring supermarkets. In an Oakland location, canned food and frozen turkeys were thrown back and forth and there were scores of injuries. An incredible service claim of $100.000 was made by a small Black Muslims bakery, and paid. Much was pilfered by the "volunteers" who bagged the produce. In San Francisco some of the thefts were on a grand scale At one distribution location, almost a hundred thousand dollars worth of food was burglarized overnight, and a truck carrying fifty thousand dollars worth of fresh meat was mysteriously emptied en route to its destined distribution point. Since no identification was required, and no policing permitted, thousands of individuals were able to collect one sack after another.

Many recipients sold off their food, and sacks of the Hearst ransom were to be had for a few dollars apiece in the streets and parks.

A. Ludlow Kramer, whose authority was now eclipsed by the power of the Coalition and its leading figure, Arnold Townsend, continued to make terse statements about the success of the program. In particular, he reiterated that PIN was operating in the spirit of the demands of the SLA. and that its efforts were hastening the release of Patricia Hearst. His name, and his program, gradually became a joke to articulate Bay Area people. Meanwhile, predictably, "the poor" and "the people" who came to claim the bags of food were losing their respectability. This development unfairly hurt all Black people in the eyes of other citizens. The program had now become a basically Black program, and since it looked bad Blacks also looked bad.

On March 9, after their long silence, the Symbionese sent forth a three-part communication, their longest one, in order to mark the end of this phase of the contest. The three parts of this tape, reprinted as the next three screeds, included a long diatribe by a new voice, "General Genina", a long supporting diatribe by Patricia Hearst, and a medley of chant-like messages by Marshal Cinque and two faked Black female voices. The pressures on the SLA were by now very serious. Their programs were going badly, their clients "the poor" and "the people" had lost face, and the attention of the media was steadily dwindling. The careful production and meticulous delivery of their new messages reveal a real dread of losing everything.

Three separate copies of the tapes were delivered. One was of bad quality, and one may have gotten into the wrong hands. For the very first time, the SLA felt forced to follow their transmission with a covering explanation.

This is Information and Intelligence Unit Four. On March 9, 1974, this unit was directed to deliver a taped communique to the news media.

Due to intelligence reports received by the federation in regards to FBI attempts to intercept and suppress any communications between the SLA and the people, a double decoy system was set up.

One tape with a gasoline credit card was sent to radio station KDIA Oakland, and another tape enclosed with an automobile credit card was sent to KSAN. We of Unit Four notified KDIA first as to the location of this tape, which allowed one of two things to happen:

Either KDIA, without telling the public or the Hearst family,turned it over to FBI who in turn suppressed it, keeping it from the Hearst family and public, or the FBI intercepted it before
KDIA got it and suppressed it from getting to the Hearst family and the public.

In any event, this allowed the second tape to get through to KSAN, because the FBI thought that the tape they had already intercepted was the only one sent out.

We of Unit Four are sending our copy of the tape because it is more audible. Please pass it along.

SCREED NINETEEN

GENINA'S TREATISE ON BREAKING OFF

Screed 18, with its peremptory demands and its tone of scorn and hatred, was not really answerable. Randolph Hearst's reply was brief and dignified. The size of the latest demand of the SLA is far beyond my financial capability, he said. Therefore the matter is now out of my hands. His associate, Charles Gould, followed him to the platform and promised the SLA and the army of reporters that the Hearst Corporation would provide the additional four million dollars, but only provided Patricia Hearst is released unharmed. And he added that no other funds will be committed. . . under any circumstances.

In their stance as a separate government, the SLA screeds people had several times threatened to "break off negotiations" or "suspend communications". Now, faced with a hard line for the first time, they carried out the threat. The three screeds in the tape of March 9 sum up and punctuate all earlier transactions, while setting forth a new line too irrational and unbelievable to be answered at all, and making new demands. Wilder, fuller, and more poetic than any other set, they mark a final departure from the forms of reason and discourse. The first and longest of them, our Screed 19, carries the voice of "General Genina", speaking for the Army and the Court of the People. Genina's voice faked that of a moderately literate Black woman in her twenties.

General Genina's long discourse covers the whole range of SLA anxieties at this late stage of the Hearst operation. Her first theme is isolation. The small Black Liberation Army and a few still weaker groups had publicly saluted the SLA, but scores or hundreds of other racial and Left groups, including all the more active ones, had denounced it as a disaster and an enemy of the Left. Genina begins with a plea for the understanding and support of all such organizations. In her second movement, with extreme detail and verve, she justifies, the present suspension of communication and negotiation, on the basis of Hearstian trickery and deceit, with special attention to the indignities the Hearst or PIN food program had visited on "the people".

In her third movement, expanding on this, Genina compares the "strategies" of the SLA and its Hearst-FBI enemies. Here, in recurring to the deeds of Mrs. Hearst as Trustee of the University of California, Genina made an effort to get back to the normal Berkeley Left issues from which Symbionism had sprouted only nine months earlier. For if the SLA had corrupted the media, the media had also corrupted the SLA, and the side-show free-food reportage was now forcing all political issues, including the basic issues of terrorism and revolution, away from the center of the stage.

In the more direful fourth and fifth parts, Genina comes to the particular case of Patricia Hearst. More emphatically than ever before, she links the destiny of Miss Hearst with the destiny of the SLA soldiers Russell and Little. The hope of getting the SLA onto a national television show had been growing in both SLA and media circles. It had been pounded at daily by reporters, by attorneys for the two men, and even by Randolph Hearst, who still hoped that appeasement of the Symbionese would help toward return of his daughter.

To those who bear the hopes and future of the people, let the voice of their guns express the words of freedom.

Greetings to the people and comrade sisters and brothers. My name is Genina and I am a general in the Symbionese Liberation Army.

I am speaking to you on behalf of the Symbionese War Council, the Court of the People, and on behalf of the Symbionese federation as a whole.

[I]

I speak the deepest expression of freedom and cry out for revolutionary unity. With profound love we greet the Black Liberation Army, the Weather Underground, the BGF and WO and those brave women and men who by force of arms have shown that there is no compromise for freedom, and that the meaning of the Federation's codes of unity holds the truth: That to die a race and be born a nation is to become free.

There have been many on the left who, without a clear understanding, have condemned the actions of the SLA and the people's forces who have chosen to fight rather than talk. These speakers condemn without clearly recognizing that our actions are a direct response to the vicious and murderous actions of the enemy corporate state against the people.

It has been claimed that we are destroying the Left but in truth an unarmed and nonfighting Left is doomed, as the people of Chile can sadly testify. The analysis of these so-called leaders who presume to speak for the people can be traced to one of two qualities: Either they are cowards afraid of revolutionary violence because it is a direct threat to their personal security or they are opportunists who have personal gains in allowing the enemy to enslave or oppress and tranquilize the people.

The dream, and indeed it is a dream, of this reactionary leadership is that the enemy corporate state will willingly give the stolen riches of the earth back to the people and that this will be accomplished through compromising talk and empty words.

In reality, the enemy state forces the people to buy back the goods that the people themselves have produced at the price of blood. To this, our bullets scream loudly. The enemy's bloodthirsty greed will be destroyed by the growing spirit of the people and their thirst for freedom.

The actions of the SLA are based on a clear understanding and analysis of the enemy and its actions against the lives and freedom of the people. We call upon the people to judge for themselves whether our tactics of waging struggle are correct or incorrect in fighting the enemy by any means necessary.

[II]

The SLA and the Court of the People wish to state to the people the reasons behind the present suspension of communications and negotiations.

The people have been experiencing the true meaning of the Hearst empire's sincerity, that true meaning being deception and lies. Throughout the previous period of communication between the SLA and the Hearst empire, the SLA and the Court of the People have dealt truthfully with all concerned. We have at all times followed our revolutionary principles of utilizing our three weapons of war: Our guns, our determination, and the truth. And this means that we will never say anything that we do not totally mean to do.

We wish to place before the people a comparison of the sincere actions of the SLA and the counter-actions of the Hearst empire.

1. The Court of the People requested that all documents of the Court be printed in full [inaudible]. The Hearst empire omitted Communiques One and Two concerning the Foster operations and Court documents that were to be published. Also the meaning of the seven-headed cobra on the reverse side of the document showing the emblem of the SLA was purposely omitted.

2. The Court of the People requested that $70 worth of top quality food, including an equal balance of drystuffs and canned goods and fresh meat, poultry, produce and dairy products, be given to poor families and in various Bay Area communities as a gesture of good faith so that negotiations for Patricia Hearst might begin. But Hearst and the Hearst empire contributed $2 million to People in Need, a program set up by Hearst in reaction to the request of the SLA. Instead of issuing a type and quality of food stipulated, PIN showed contempt for the people through disorganization in distribution of surplus commodities instead of top quality fresh meats, vegetables and produce. PIN also intended to shame the people by trying to distribute hog feed instead of top quality drystuffs. The people had to stand in long lines

for hours only to be treated as dogs when the PIN food was thrown at them. Many people were injured by police in East Oakland.

3 .The SLA showed severe displeasure with the meager Hearst contribution and with the Hearst PIN program. The SLA reissued its guidelines for an adequate and equitable food distribution and requested that the Hearst empire add an additional $4 million to the measly $2 million. In a communique the SLA proved the Hearst trickery by stating just how rich and powerful the Hearsts and the Hearst empire really are. Randolph Hearst responded deceitfully that he could not meet financially the SLA requests, and stated in typical capitalist fashion that the situation was out of his hands. As if Hearst had no connection with the Hearst Corporation, the corporation, supposedly out of the kindness of its corporate heart, responded that it would provide the additional $4 million, but only after Patricia Hearst is released.

Hearst and the Hearst Corporation assumed that the SLA and the people were inexperienced in the area of corporate trickery, and so they said that they would give $2 million upon Patricia Hearst's release and the rest in January, 1975. However, the people have experienced such trickery too many times in the past to ever be fooled by it again. SLA elements were at Wounded Knee and we too honored the elders' decision to cease the occupation. But we will not forget the lesson that we learned from our brothers and sisters there: One thing above all, never trust the words of the enemy.

Hearst's PIN program stated that it would follow the SLA distribution guidelines. However, instead of $70 worth of top quality food, the people have gotten $8 worth of mediocre food. Instead of fresh meat, half the people received one chicken. Many stood in long, cold lines for only a bag full of cabbages, while others stood in line and got nothing at all.

PIN said it distributed 30,000 bags of food. But this lie was revealed by WAPAC and the Coalition, which said only 15,000 walked away with food. After the second day of food distribution, WAPAC and the Coalition issued their reports on Hearst's PIN program.

The SLA and the Court of the People and the People themselves want to see this report printed in full in all forms of the media. There has never been any uncensored, uncut media reporting of any statement made by the Coalition speakers. Ludlow Kramer has boasted the well-known lies that Hearst's program has carried out the terms of the LA-prescribed good faith gesture. The people know his words don't make no bag of cabbages into meat. [sic]

[III]

The Court of the People have a clear understanding of the actions of the Hearsts and the Hearst empire as a whole, in regards to its deceit and silence concerning its interests and crimes against the people.

It is no surprise that Mrs. Hearst has never once said anything about her activities on the University of California Board of Regents and its policy of financing corporations who [sic] operate internationally and exploit the hungry and oppressed people of the earth.

It is no coincidence that Mr. Hearst remained silent about his vast interest in the Safeway Stores, Inc., and Exxon, because it is very important that the people of this country not ask questions about these interests.

It is very important to the enemy that people do not begin to question why it is that the man who is so concerned for bilingual education for Chicano people is also the same man who owns vast stock interests in Safeway Stores, Inc., and thousands of acres of land robbed from Chicano people in California. And a silver mine and thousands of acres of land in Mexico that the Hearst empire has exploited from the peoples in Mexico.

Mr. and Mrs. Hearst, by constantly maintaining the secure position where they are not forced to reveal their interests and crimes, and without really conceding anything to the people, hope to gain the release of the prisoner.

In our analysis of enemy strategy we find multiple reasons for why [sic] the Hearst empire has not complied with our request.

1. By frustrating the people, forcing them to continually return to food distribution centers, stand in long lines and receive $8 worth of food, the Hearst empire attempted to discredit the political point of the action.

2. By handing out surplus and low grade donated food, some of which was not even meant for human consumption, in an undignified manner, the Hearst empire attempted to discredit and disprove the example we intended to display.

3. By prolonging the program, soliciting donations and giving nowhere near the required amount, the Hearst empire could retain control under the facade of humanitarianism with no loss to their bank books.

The tactics of misplaced supply of the food, delayed and missing trucks, supposed hijackings of mysterious trucks claimed to be loaded with top quality meat, are all designed to mislead the people into believing that these things were normal mishaps and that the Hearst empire was not responsible for them and was really attempting to meet some of the needs of the people. The Hearst empire has attempted to encourage division among the people by giving them crumbs to fight over.

Our strategy was to show by example what can be done: That this goodwill gesture was intended to give some food to the people, while at the same time pointing out our understanding that the people can never expect the enemy to feed them. That, in fact, the people do not want the enemy to feed them, but rather the people must have back their land and control over their ow~ :~ destinies and must themselves realize the fruits of their own labor.

We did this to point out how the enemy can easily afford to feed the people if it were forced to, but what the enemy cannot afford is to reveal to the people the total extent of the sum of the wealth that it has robbed from the people.

[IV]

The SLA stated that Patricia Campbell Hearst would be kept in accordance with international codes of war regarding prisoners of war, and that she would be maintained in protective custody. It was further stated that the captive SLA elements who stay at San Quentin would also have to be kept in accordance with such codes because of their legal POW status.

The SLA requested that Randolph and Catherine Hearst and the Hearst empire see to it that our comrades' conditions follow those guidelines It was stated at that time that Patricia Hearst's condition would correspond at all times with that of the captured brothers The SLA has waited with disciplined patience for the agents of the fascist state, including the Hearst media empire to deal with the conditions of our comrades' confinement.

The Symbionese War Council, the Court of the People, had considered transferring Patricia Campbell Hearst to a security area which would physically correspond to a strip cell on Death Row m San Quentin concentration camp. This would be an obvious response to barbaric conditions which our comrades are forced to endure.

However, after extensive nationwide intelligence and analysis by the Symbionese War Council, it became clear that the fascist corporate state and its chief domestic police agency, the FBI, and 4 other police state agencies and institutions, intended to set up Patricia Hearst for execution in order to discredit and isolate the people's forces.

This is shown by the deliberate disregard for the health, life and safety of Joseph Remiro and Russell Little, and the plans of the police state agencies to see to it that Patricia Hearst is killed.

Despite FBI claims that they would not do anything to endanger Patricia Hearst's life, they have raided homes throughout the country knowing full well that to do so would endanger the life of Patricia Hearst.

The plans of the police state agency are to see to it that Patricia Hearst is killed and then use her death to further rally middle America in support of the Nixon-represented corporate dictatorship and against all revolutionary forces.

The fascist state and the FBI have attempted to manipulate public opinion in support of Patricia Hearst's safety and eventual return while at the same time creating conditions that it knows would force her execution, saving them the embarrassment of doing it themselves.

But, we have repeatedly stated that Patricia Hearst's safety, execution or freedom is totally her family's and its class's responsibility.

It is in the direct interest of the fascist corporate state to eliminate all popular revolutionary forces, even if that would mean sending the FBI to execute Patricia Hearst.

U.S. Attorney General William Saxbe's statement that the FBI should bust in [sic] to rescue the prisoner was no slip of the tongue, but was in reality a prematurely exposed government policy decision.

Just as Nelson Rockefeller and the prison authorities in New York State could easily sacrifice the lives of hostage correctional officers at Attica in order to kill incarcerated freedom fighters inside, just as Ronald Reagan and prison authorities in California could sacrifice the life of Judge Haley at the Marin County Courthouse in order to kill manchild Jonathan Jackson and incarcerated freedom fighters from San Quentin, so, too, can the U.S. government and the FBI, with the sick permission of her father, willingly and without regret sacrifice the life of Patricia Hearst in order to attempt to kill members of the Symbionese Liberation Army.

We know from our experiences in prisons, and from our comrades who have been killed in prisons, and from all those comrades still locked down, Russell Little and Joseph Remiro have already been issued tickets to ride the fascist corporate state's railroad to the gas chamber, and that the appointment by Randolph Hearst of a member of the fascist U.C. Board of Regents to insure so-called due process of law, is merely a ploy to hide the already predetermined destination of that train, not to stop it.

[V]

In response to Randolph Hearst's public request that Patricia Hearst be allowed to communicate periodically with her family in conjunction with international codes of war regarding prisoners of war, the SLA asks Randolph Hearst:

On what basis should the people's forces allow such communications?

1. The Symbionese War Council has determined that communication between POW Patricia Hearst and her family will come after the immediate creation of the necessary mechanisms whereby Russell Little and Joseph Remiro can communicate via live national TV with the people and the SLA concerning the full scope of their physical health and all the conditions of their confinement.

2. That this tape and a transcript of it be published in full, omitting nothing, in all forms of the media.

SCREED TWENTY

PATRICIA HEARST'S SLA TESTAMENT

Patricia Hearst's part in the termination of negotiations came as a shock to many people. Her taped message, Screed 20, is a sweeping and often startling document. She spoke it ad libitum, but obviously following noted-down headings in a clear, earnest, serious voice, with no sign of tension and certainly no sign of rebellion.

The contents of the screed closely echo and sometimes amplify the ideas of General Genina's analytical paper, Screed 19. Like Genina, Miss Hearst demanded that Remiro and Little be given their television hour. Like Genina also, she argued that her father had deliberately lied about his resources, sabotaged the free-food program, and allied himself with the FBI in such a way as to endanger her life. And like Genina, she tried to get back to staple Berkeley issues such as her mother's performance on the University Board of Regents. What was more startling than all of this was Patricia Hearst's suggestion that she was, or was becoming, a Symbionese soldier herself. Her statement about a shotgun and "cyanide buckshot" to be used by her in case of an FBI attack carried this idea as far as possible. It was now "only the FBI and certain people in government" whom she recognized as enemies.

From the first hours of the kidnapping, more than a month earlier, rumors that Patricia Hearst was an SLA sympathizer, and had helped to engineer her own abduction, had circulated through Black and Left circles in Berkeley and San Francisco. Screed 20 intensified and spread these rumors, and they began to be mentioned even in the press. The breaking off of communications between Hearst and the SLA left the question open.

Mom, Dad:

I received the message you broadcast last Sunday. It was good to hear from you after so much silence. But what you had to say sounded like you don't care if I ever get out of here. All you want is to hear from me sometimes. Your silence definitely jeopardized my safety because it allows the FBI to continue to attempt to find me, and Governor Reagan to make antagonistic statements, with no response from you.

I'm beginning to feel that the FBI would rather that I get killed. I'm telling you this now because I don't think the FBI will let any more words from me get through to the media. I hear that people all around the country keep calling on the SLA to release me unharmed. But the SLA are not the ones who are harming me. It's the FBI, along with your indifference to the poor, and your failure to deal with the people and the SLA in a meaningful, fair way.

I don't believe you're doing everything you can, everything in your power. I don't believe that you're doing anything at all. You said it was out of your hands; what you should have said was that you wash your hands of it.

I guess that you don't think, or understand, that it is not just the crimes of you and mom personally that I am being held for, but the crimes of the University of California Board of Regents, and your voting record, Mom, when you were on that board. And also the crimes of the Hearst Corporation.

Dad, you can't put the responsibility for my status on the corporation. You seem to be ignoring the fact that you are the chairman of the board and Uncle Bill is president of the Hearst Corporation. I know that if anything happens to me, it will be because your corporation advisers and the FBI decided to protect their interests instead of my life.

I don't know who influences you to not comply with the good faith gesture. I know that you could have done it the way the SLA asked. I mean I know that we have enough money. But it seems to me that you told the FBI to do whatever they decide is necessary to destroy the SLA. But it's becoming true [ie, clear?] J, Dad.

[II]

I've heard the reports concerning the FBI investigation and interrogations, Governor Reagan's careless and antagonistic remarks, and the attempt of federal agencies to maneuver the news media to mentally prepare the public for my death,calling for mass prayers and petitions to the SLA for my release.

From this I am forced to draw only one conclusion, that the FBI and other federal agencies want me to die. I no longer seem to have any importance as a human being; rather, I have become all-important as a political pivot point for certain right wing elements. And I can only be used successfully by these people if I am killed.

As for the constant reassurances by the FBI that my safety is their primary concern, I can only say that the FBI has never been famous for its concern for the safety of hostages. From what I've seen so far this case is no different.

Whether consciously or not, the news media has [sic] been assisting the FBI for its now overt attempts to set me up for execution. It has done this primarily in two ways.

First, by promoting a public image of my father as a bereaved parent who has done all he can to meet the demands of his daughter's kidnappers, and who now awaits her supposedly long overdue release. In fact, the SLA demands have not even been approximated, and they have made it very clear that until the good faith gesture is completed, negotiations for my release will not begin.

Second, the media, with cooperation from my parents, has [sic] created a public image of me as a helpless innocent girl who was supposedly abducted by two terrible Blacks, escaped convicts. I'm a strong woman and I resent being used in this way.

[III]

I have been hearing reports about the food program. So far it sounds like you and your advisers have managed to turn it into a real disaster.

I heard only 15,000 people received food in the first two weeks and that each of them received only about $8 worth. It sounds like most of the food is of low quality. No one received any beef or lamb, and it certainly didn't sound like the kind of food our family is used to eating.

The SLA wanted this program to be over in one month. They wanted each person to get $70 worth of good food all at once. If you'd just done what the SLA wanted for the food program, the month would almost be over and I would be ready to get out of here.

What you've done is tell People in Need to set up this program where people get at most an $8 bag of food, so it's being stretched out; and [but?] it's a really discouraging thing for people who need food.

Dad, I know that you got most of the food donated for People in Need. And you have put very little money at all into the program.

[IV]

Mom, I can't believe that you've agreed with the "out of my hands" stance of Daddy's program.

I just wish that you could be stronger and pull yourself together from all these emotional outbursts and see if you can persuade Dad to listen to you and the rest of the family. Mom, you've got to stand up and speak for yourself. You seem to be allowing other people to make your decisions.

Your statements, if I can call them that, have given the FBI the go-ahead to kill me. I wish God would touch your heart and get you to do something concrete to help me.

I wish I knew what the rest of the family was thinking and saying. It's hard to believe that my sisters and cousins aren't saying anything.

If it had been you, Mom, or you, Dad, who had been kidnapped instead of me, I know that I and the rest of the family and your friends would do anything to get you back. It could have been one of you and how would you feel if you had been written off the way I seem to have been?

I'm starting to think that no one is concerned about me any more. I wish that I could hear from the rest of the family. I'd like to hear what my sisters have to say about Dad's decision not to comply with the terms of the good faith gesture.

Steven, what do you have to say? Willy, I know you really care about what happens to me. Make Dad let you talk. You can't be silent.

Everyone who hears this tape, I hope you will believe me and not think that I've been brainwashed or tortured into saying this. Please listen to me because I'm speaking honestly and from the heart.

In the last week it has become obvious to the SLA and all hungry people, and to me, that my father is not even attempting to show a gesture of good faith. I guess that everybody knows that is why there's been no further word from the SLA about negotiating for my release.

[V]

In the last few days members of the Federation have spoken with me. They have given me some newspaper reports to read about the current practices of psycho-surgery and the use, daily, of drugs and tranquilizers in prisons throughout the country. I have also been given some journals commentaries about kinds of conditions that exist in prisons in general and in the adjustment center at San Quentin in particular.

Members of the Federation have also given me a choice of books to read. I have been reading a book by George Jackson called "Blood in My Eye". I'm starting to understand what he means when he talks about fascism in America.

Joseph Remiro and Russell Little, the two men in San Quentin, haven't even come to trial yet, and already they are being held in strip cells on death row. It's really hard to believe that such an obvious violation of the Constitution is taking place, but it's true. How can people think that these men can get a fair trial? Can there be any doubt in people's minds as to what the verdict will be?

Members of the Federation are studying intelligence reports gathered by the SLA on the activities of the FBI. These, combined with discussions the members of the Federation have had with me, and my own observations of the way my father has been conducting himself, have made me afraid; because I realize that the plans are coming from the FBI and the Attorney General's office in Washington to execute the two men in San Quentin. Or if that cannot be swiftly accomplished, to execute me by seeing to it that even if I am released I will not get home alive. Or by attempting to raid this place where I am being held, and then [to] discredit the SLA by saying that they were the ones who killed me.

Because of these dangers, I have been transferred to a special security unit of the SLA combat forces, where I am being held in protective custody. I have been issued a 12-gauge riot shotgun and I have been receiving instructions on how to use it.

While I have no access to ammunition, in the event of an attack by the FBI, I have been told that I will be given an issue of cyanide buckshot in order to protect myself. Because it is the Federation's opinion, and my own from observation, that if the FBI does rush in, they will obviously be doing it against the wishes of my family and in total disregard for my safety. In fact, they would be doing it to murder me.

Under international codes of war I am allowed to communicate with members of my family, and because of the scope of this incident with the public as well. However, I should tell you that the practice of allowing me to communicate with you will not continue until the SLA hears from the two men at San Quentin. They want to hear what the two men have to say in a live nationwide broadcast, so they can hear all the conditions of their confinement.

I really want to get out of here and I really want to get home alive. I am appealing to the public and asking them not to assist the FBI in their investigation. Doing so is simply helping them to dig my grave. And I ask those people who say they pray for me and those who sign petitions to the SLA for my safe release to redirect their energies into opposing the FBI's brutal attempts to murder me and the two men in San Quentin.

I no longer fear the SLA, because they are not the ones who want me to die. The SLA want to feed the people, and assure safety and justice for the two men at San Quentin. I realize now it is the FBI who [sic] want to murder me. Only the FBI and certain people in the government stand to gain anything by my death.

SCREED TWENTY ONE

THREE LAST WORDS, FOR WAR

Sent in with the two previous screeds, and obviously meant as an inspirational peroration suitable for closing out the series, was a three-part chant or recitativo. Two of the voices were those of unidentified SLA officers, both young females. The concluding passage featured the well-known voice of Field Marshal Cinque, otherwise DeFreeze. The readings were from scripts, and were done with a conscious projection of emotional tones. The women counterfeited Black accents.

It is impossible to say when the screed was composed. Its great generalization, and its failure to mention the Hearsts, the food program, or the imprisoned SLA soldiers, suggest that it was an old production put together when the SLA was still in its oratorical Berkeley Left stage of development. One can surmise that as they broke off their negotiations and began the new period of silence, the Symbionese went through the files for a suitable last word, or parting shot.

Voice of a Woman Soldier

A warning to the fascist military corporate state:

We have declared revolutionary war upon you, the enemy of the people, and our seriousness and determination will not be swayed by any number of your U.S. government-inspected super-pigs. For those that you have hunted are now hunting you.

Death to the fascist insect that preys upon the life of the people.

Voice of a Second Woman Soldier

Comrade sisters, resistance fighters, we greet you and call you to arms in the struggle to free all the people.

Today our daughters and our sons, our mothers and our fathers, stand with the people in the fight for true freedom for all people. No people are free until we are all free.

We women know the truth as it has been revealed in our own lives. We turn our rage toward the enemy in a direct line, down the sights of our guns. We must turn our anger towards those who profit off our suffering, and have our anger be reflected in military tactics that utilize people's violence against the men and women who are the monsters of capitalist violence.

Until we meet in the streets may we have a strong back, like that of the grave digger.

The Closing, by Cinque

This is General Field Marshal Cinque in command. I would like to take the opportunity to speak to my people and all the people, and to those who I fight against who prey upon the lives of our children.

Black people must come together and stop robbing and oppressing each other and all oppressed people. It is time that black people understand that the enemy is not white, brown or black people.

The oppressor is not a particular color. The oppressor is a system and the corporate ruling class that preys upon the lives of all people.

I call upon oppressed people of all colors to arm themselves in defense of their own freedom while they still have the chance.

I call upon the robbers, pimps, the drug addicts, the prostitutes, and all those who have been used as pawns against the people, to turn their rage and violence toward the true enemy of the people, the corporate ruling class.

I call upon the people to shed no more blood of the innocent but rather bring death to the makers of fear, and those that deceive us into fighting amongst ourselves because of our different colors.

I call upon our mothers and fathers to hear the voice that rings in our hearts for freedom.

I call upon them to hear the cries of our children being murdered in the streets, and to understand that there is no compromise for freedom.

I call upon the people to join the Federation. And that only means one thing: that is, by answering this call to arms with the sounds of your guns and your commitment to save the children.

SCREED TWENTY-TWO

THE APRIL FOOL COMMUNIQUE

Patricia Hearst's diatribe against her family and the "corporate fascist state" was read over many radio and television stations and published in many newspapers. It caused a new burst of headline publicity, and gave many more people, especially among non-white political and pressure groups, a chance to compete for star billing with the media.

The reactions of men and women who had already gotten into the picture were predictable. The Hearsts, Steven Weed, A. Ludlow Kra and the shoguns of WAPAC and the other Coalition groups, still p fessed to believe that they could do business with the SLA. Under premise, they organized a massive shift in the character of the Hearst PIN food program. Kramer's social-service dream of a "supplemental" and "ongoing" foundation which would help thousands of hard-pressed families over many years was abandoned in favor of the big-party one-scramble, food dream of the SLA. About one million dollars ha been disbursed from Hearst's original gift; the new idea was to spend the rest in a single distribution.

One million dollars worth of high-quality food was accordingly assembled, packed into cartons stamped with the SLA snake, and shoved forth from seventeen distribution points. Once again the chief beneficiaries were Blacks, for by now collection of the Hearst food had become a sort of ghetto game. There was heavier pilferage than ever before, and great deal of new violence, as well as some bad feeling between the races. It was particularly noticed that whole families of Blacks would enter lines, so that one group might collect six or eight of the forty-pound boxes, and that many individuals and families drove from point to point, filling their trucks or automobiles during the course of the day. This practice was especially noticed in Chinatown. Oriental organizations had opposed the food plan from the beginning, and refused to take any part in it. Their spokesmen now hastened to point out that the food distributed at the Church of Our Lady of Guadalupe, the Chinatown distribution point, went almost entirely to "other races" who had invaded the district for the one day.

When the second' million was gone, Kramer and his staff went back to their homes in Washington State. Fearing violence in the PIN head-quarters, the PIN head gave his final news conference in a downtown hotel. Kramer was by then embittered. According to him, the program had been run in "an atmosphere of violence" from its beginning. He averred that most of the people who had dealt with the PIN had done so for selfish reasons, as a means of acquiring publicity and power in their communities, and alluded to simple thefts and hijackings amounting to hundreds of thousands of dollars. In his reports, however, just as in the reports of the Coalition leaders, it was stressed that so far as the means went, the sudden-shower food demand of the SLA had been met. If the SLA agreed, it did not say so. Its silence continued for a nerve-racking three weeks.

The heavy reportage of these three weeks was mostly by way of personalia. Radicals, criminals, professors, psychiatrists, and leaders of the various minority groups were interviewed, gave their theories, and enjoyed their little day of fame. The issue of Remiro and Little also made heavy news. Though denied their national television show, and duly indicted for the murder of Foster, the two SLA soldiers joined those who theorized the situation, and issued a string of manifestos and communiques of their own.

Randolph Hearst and the Hearst Corporation completed the ransom arrangements by putting another four million dollars in escrow, to be used for the SLA or PIN programs, but only on the condition that Patricia Hearst be actually released. Though the Hearsts, Weed, and the run of radical and militant spokesmen still hoped for peace with the SLA, and for the happy return of Miss Hearst, the concept of mere good-will gestures was now worn out.

On April 1st the SLA leader, Cinque, broke his long silence. This time he sent his message through a sex-oriented counter-culture newspaper, the San Francisco Phoenix, with a bouquet of roses. The Phoenix had been honored in this way because of the long "interview with the SLA" which it had published the week before. John Bryan, the editor of the Phoenix, now rose to stardom, and was photographed with the Hearsts and widely interviewed. "It is," he said in wonder, "the greatest scoop of my career". The article which had so impressed the SLA turned out, however, to have been a cruel hoax of his own. Short of copy for the Phoenix, Bryan had concocted the whole interview himself. But the message, this time a typed one labeled "Communique No. 7," was real enough.

[Transmittal to the Phoenix]

This communication is to be sent through you to the people. You are hereby directed by the Court of the People to notify immediately radio stations KPFA, KSAN and KDIA concerning the complete contents of this communication, understanding that you must not cooperate with the FBI by turning over this communication or by providing them with any information.

Protect your rights as reporters by refusing to reveal your sources of information.

Communique No. 7
March 29, 1974
Symbionese Liberation Army, Information and Intelligence Unit No. 4
Court Order: Release of the Codes of War of the SLA.
Subject: negotiations and release of the prisoner.
Court Order issued by the Court of people.

Herein enclosed are the Codes of War of the Symbionese Liberation Army, these documents as all SLA documents are to be printed in full and omitting nothing by order of this court in all, forms of the media. Further communications regarding subject prisoner will follow in the following 72 hours. Communications will state the state [sic], city and time of release of the prisoner.

Signed:1.1. Unit 4
General Field Marshall Cin SLA

SCREED TWENTY THREE

THE SYMBIONESE CODES OF WAR

The April Fool's Day message, Screed 22, drew the expected avalanche of headline reportage.

Deliberately misreading its text, Hearst, Mrs. Hearst, Weed, and the various experts professed to interpret it as a promise to release Patricia Hearst "within the following 72 hours", and there was widespread speculation on the futile question of when the 72-hour period had begun. A great deal of self-congratulation by Coalition and PIN people reached the media at this time. It was claimed by many leaders that the new big-party giveaway had at last satisfied the SLA. Some articles in the Codes of War delivered to the Phoenix office with the April 1 message even suggested that the SLA might be breaking up through peaceful departure of its soldiers from their cells and camps.

These Codes of War, which were typed out like the covering message, are of later date than the war laws given in Screeds 3 through 7. Many of their articles apply to the circumstances which had emerged after the arrest of Remiro and Little. Oddly, most of the crimes judged worthy of "PENALTY BY DEATH" had recently been committed by key soldiers in the organization. By Little, for example, who had surrendered; by Remiro, who had "deserted a wounded comrade" before also surrendering; and by Fahizah, or Nancy Perry, who had abandoned her "cell unit" or "base camp" and its incriminating contents. Other items in the "Death" part, especially the conditions by which SLA soldiers might drop out, and the fierce warnings to "paid and unpaid informants", also related to important concerns of the moment.

Other articles in the SLA Codes of War covered the wide spectrum between small housekeeping details and the grand principles of commitment and sacrifice. More than any other screed of the SLA, the Codes of War reflect the unromantic day-to-day practical of life in a "cell" or "camp". One is sure, reading it, that its main author Field Marshal Cinque has become a troubled and worried man. Whatever else they may have been, the Berkeley young people of the SLA were disparate in type, individualistic in outlook, and messy and unsoldierly in their habits. The grand theories of the Symbionese Federation were no longer obscuring the ordinary problems of group law and discipline.

CODES OF WAR OF THE UNITED SYMBIONESE LIBERATION ARMY

PENALTY BY DEATH

ALL CHARGES THAT FACE A DEATH PENALTY SHALL BE PRESENTED TO A JURY TRIAL MADE UP OF THE MEMBERS OF THE GUERRILLA FORCES. THE JURY SHALL BE SELECTED BY THE CHARGED AND THE JUDGE CONDUCTING THE TRIAL SHALL BE SELECTED BY THE CHARGED ALSO. THE CHARGED SHALL SELECT HIS OR HER DEFENSE, AND THE TRIAL JUDGE SHALL

SELECT THE PROSECUTOR. THE JURY SHALL NUMBER AT
LEAST 3/4THS OF THE REMAINING MEMBERS OF THE CELLS,
AND THE VERDICT MUST BE UNANIMOUS.

1. THE SURRENDER TO THE ENEMY.

2. THE KILLING OF A COMRADE OR DISOBEYING ORDERS THAT
RESULT IN THE DEATH OF A COMRADE.

3. THE DESERTING OF A COMRADE ON THE FIELD OF WAR.

a. LEAVING A TEAM POSITION, THEREBY NOT COVERING A
COMRADE.

b. LEAVING A WOUNDED COMRADE.

4. THE INFORMING TO THE ENEMY OR SPYING AGAINST THE
PEOPLE OR GUERRILLAS.

5. LEAVING A CELL UNIT OR BASE CAMP WITHOUT ORDERS.

Any comrade may leave the guerrilla forces if she or he feels that they no
longer feel the courage or faith in the people and the struggle that we wage.
A comrade, however, must follow the CODES OF WAR in doing this: that
is, he or she must inform the commanding guerrilla of their wish to go from
guerrilla force. Thereupon, the guerrilla in command will release them in a
safe area. The excombatants may only leave with his or her personal side-arm.
REMEMBER, this is the ONLY way a comrade may leave the S.L.A., any
other way is deserting, punishable by death.

6. ALL PAID OR UNPAID INFORMANTS OPERATING WITHIN
THE COMMUNITY AGAINST THE PEOPLE AND THE GUERRIL-
LA FORCES ARE SENTENCED WITHOUT TRIAL! TO IMMEDIATE
DEATH.

PENALTY BY DISCIPLINARY ACTION

DISCIPLINARY ACTION SHOULD BE PRIMARILY TO AID THE
COLLECTIVE GROWTH OF THE CELL, SO THAT. THROUGH POS-
ITIVE ACTION THE MISTAKE IS UNDERSTOOD, ALL CHARGES

THAT FACE DISCIPLINARY ACTION SHALL BE UNDER THE FULL
CONTROL OF THE GUERRILLA IN COMMAND, AND SHE OR HE
SHALL WEIGH ALL I EVIDENCE AND SHALL DECIDE THE VER-
DICT, AND IF NEEDED, DIRECT THE DISCIPLINARY ACTION TO
BE TAKEN BY THE CHARGED COMRADE NECESSARY TO DIRECT
HIM OR HER. EXAMPLES OF DISCIPLINARY ACTION ARE
THE CLEANING AND MAINTENANCE OF ALL CELL ARMS, AM-
MUNITION AND EXPLOSIVES FOR ONE WEEK, THE UPKEEP
OF OUTHOUSES, THE FULL SUSPENSION OF WINE AND CIGA-
RETTES, AND EXTRA DUTIES SUCH AS   ADDITIONAL WATCH-
ES, PRACTICE AND STUDY PERIODS, CORRESPONDENCE, FIL-
ING, TYPING, WASHING, CLEANING, COOKING, AND PHYSICAL
EXERCISES.

1. LACK OF RESPONSIBILITY AND DETERMINED ~ DECISIVE-
NESS IN FOLLOWING ORDERS.

2. NONVIGILANCE OR THE LEAVING OF AN ASSIGNED POST
WITHOUT ORDERS.

3. LACK OF RESPONSIBILITY IN MAINTAINING EQUIPMENT OR
PROFICIENCY IN ALL GUERRILLA SKILLS, ESPECIALLY SHOOT-
ING.

4. THE USE OF ANY UNMEDICALLY PRESCRIBED DRUG. THIS
RULE RELATES TO THE US& OF SUCH DRUGS AS HEROIN,
SPEED, PEYOTE, MESCALINE, REDS, PEP PILLS, WHITES, YELLOW
JACKETS, BENNIES, DEXIES, GOOF BALLS, LSD, AND ANY OTH-
ER KIND OF HALLUCINARY DRUGS. HOWEVER, PERMISSION
IS GRANTED FOR THE USE OF ONLY TWO TYPES OF RELAXING
DRUGS: THESE ARE MARIJUANA, AND/OR BEER AND WINE AND
OTHER ALCOHOL. THIS PERMISSION IS ONLY GRANTED WHEN
APPROVED BY THE GUERRILLA IN COMMAND, AND WITH VERY
RESTRAINING USE ONLY. NO OFFICER MAY GRANT THE USE OF
ANY OF THESE SAID DRUGS TO THE FULL NUMBER OF FORC-
ES UNDER HIS OR HER COMMAND. IF THIS PERMISSION IS
GRANTED ONLY HALF THE FORCE WILL BE ALLOWED TO TAKE
PART, WHILE THE OTHER HALF WILL STAND GUARD DUTY.
THE PAST HAS SHOWN ONCE TRUE REVOLUTIONARIES HAVE
SERIOUSLY UNDERTAKEN REVOLUTIONARY ARMS STRUGGLE,

MARIJUANA AND ALCOHOL ARE NOT USED FOR RECREATION-
AL PURPOSES OR TO DILUTE OR BLUR THE CONSCIOUSNESS
OF REALITY, BUT VERY SMALL AMOUNTS FOR MEDICINAL PUR-
POSES TO CALM NERVES UNDER TIMES OF TENSION, NOT TO
DISTORT REALITY.

5. THE FAILURE TO SEVER ALL PAST CONTACTS OR FAILING TO
DESTROY ALL EVIDENCE OF IDENTIFICATION OR ASSOCIATION.

PENALTY BY DISCIPLINARY ACTION

6. KILLING OF AN UNARMED ENEMY: IN THIS INSTANCE THE
ENEMY REFERS TO MEMBERS OF U.S.A. RANK AND FILE ONLY
AND NOT TO ANY MEMBERS OF THE CIA, FBI, OR OTHER SPE-
CIAL AGENTS OR ANY POLITICAL POLICE STATE AGENTS. MEM-
BERS OF THE USA MILITARY RANK AND FILE ARE TO BE AC-
CORDED THIS DISTINCTION BECAUSE WE RECOGNIZE THAT
MANY OF THEM HAVE BEEN FORCED INTO MEMBERSHIP EI-
THER DIRECTLY, THROUGH THE DRAFT, OR INDIRECTLY DUE
TO ECONOMIC PRESSURES.

7. TORTURES OR SEXUAL ASSAULT ON EITHER A COMRADE OR
PEOPLE OF THE ENEMY.

8. CRIMINAL ACTS AGAINST THE POOR,COMRADES OR GUER-
RILLA FORCES.

9. MALICIOUS CURSING OR ANY KIND OF DISRESPECT TO
THOSE IN COMMAND, A COMRADE, OR THE PEOPLE.

10. DECEIVING OR LYING TO FELLOW COMRADES OR THE
PEOPLE. IF ANY OF THESE ACTS ARE COMMITTED ON A CON-
TINUOUS BASIS, THE CHARGED COMRADE SHALL BECOME A
PRISONER OF THE CELL AND SHALL REMAIN IN THIS PRISON-
ER STATUS UNTIL SUCH TIME AS SHE OR HE IS ABLE TO PROVE
THEIR RENEWED COMMITMENT TO REVOLUTIONARY DISCI-
PLINE AND REVOLUTIONARY PRINCIPLES OR THE CHARGED
MAY REQUEST TO BE DISHONORABLY DISCHARGED. [sic]

CONDUCT OF GUERRILLA FORCES TOWARDS THE ENEMY SOL-

DIERS AND PRISONERS.

1. PRISONERS OF WAR SHALL BE HELD UNDER THE INTER-NATIONAL CODES OF WAR, THEY SHALL BE PROVIDED WITH ADEQUATE FOOD, MEDICAL AID, AND EXERCISES.

2. ALL USA MILITARY RANK AND FILE FORCES SHALL BE AL-LOWED TO SURRENDER UPON OUR CONDITIONS OF SURREN-DER, AND THEREUPON THEY SHALL BE CAREFULLY SEARCHED AND INTERROGATED. ALL PRISONERS ARE TO RECEIVE IN-STRUCTION ON THE GOALS OF SYMBIONESE LIBERATION ARMY, THEN RELEASED IN A SAFE AREA.

3. ALL WEAPONS, MEDICAL AND FOOD SUPPLIES, I MAPS, MILI-TARY EQUIPMENT AND MONEY ARE TO BE CONFISCATED AND TURNED INTO THE GUERRILLA IN CHARGE.

4. UNDER NO CONDITIONS SHALL ANY RANK AND FILE ENEMY SOLDIER BE RELIEVED OF HIS OR HER PERSONAL PROPERTY.

CONDUCT OF GUERRILLA FORCES TOWARDS THE PEOPLE

ALL GUERRILLA FORCES SHALL CONDUCT THEMSELVES IN A MANNER OF RESPECT TOWARD THE PEOPLE, AND SHALL WHEN ABLE AND SAFE TO DO SO, PROVIDE FOOD AND OTHER AID TO THE PEOPLE. THEY SHALL, WHEN POSSIBLE, INFORM THE PEOPLE OF THE GOALS OF THE UNITED SYMBIONESE FEDERATION AND ENCOURAGE OTHER WOMEN AND MEN TO JOIN OUR FORCES AND TO SERVE THE PEOPLE IN FIGHT FOR FREEDOM.

ALL COMRADES HAVE ONE MAIN RESPONSIBILITY, THAT IS TO STRUGGLE AND WIN AND STAND TOGETHER, SO NO COM-RADE STANDS ALONE, ALL MUST LOOK OUT FOR EACH OTH-ER, ALL MUST AID THE OTHER BLACK, BROWN, RED, YELLOW, WHITE, MAN OR WOMAN, ALL OR NONE.

THIS DOCUMENT MAY CHANGE FROM TIME TO TIME, SO OFFICERS ARE REQUESTED TO FOLLOW THE CHANGES WITH DISCIPLINE.

TO THOSE WHO WOULD BEAR THE HOPES AND FUTURE OF
THE PEOPLE LET THE VOICE OF THEIR GUNS EXPRESS THE
WORD OF FREEDOM.

Gen. Field Marshall
S.L.A.
Cin

SCREED TWENTY FOUR

A CREDO OF TEKO

Screeds 24, 25, 26, and 27 were delivered together, first as tapes, then as carbon-copy typescripts. With them was Screed 28, the strangest one of all, the final message of Patricia Hearst before her enlistment as a soldier of the SLA. This time the lucky first recipient was Radio Station KSAN, in San Francisco. There had been a gradual movement of the SLA emphasis from Berkeley to the central city. Many observers had begun to think that the central headquarters of the SLA was in the Haight-Ashbury of Western Addition, and it was often speculated that Miss Hearst herself was imprisoned there.

The astonishing new message fell into a fragile and troubled situation. Escrow arrangements for the four million new dollars had just been completed. The FBI and local police agencies were still refusing to take any positive action. Some police officers were visiting people and asking questions, but no warrants were issued and no premises searched. The Alameda County grand jury had completed its work and was ready to indict Little and Remiro for the murder of Dr. Foster, a matter which was held to be independent and unconnected to the Hearst kidnapping. Though unable to procure their national television show, Little and Remiro had begun to send their own regular communiques to favored radio stations. Meanwhile the pundits, technical experts, and old associates of SLA members ever more swiftly followed one another through the publicity system of the mass media. To all this, the hinted half-promise of the April 1st communique, and the feverish misinterpretations of its text, had added piquant new excitements. That something new and great would happen was expected everywhere.

The introductory speaker of the new packet, a soldier named Teko, led off rather gently. His contribution amounts to a general credo in which the dialectics of the Symbionese are summarized. As did earlier screeds, his communication envisages an open rising or rebellion, perhaps on the order of the race riots of the earlier 1960's, but this time directed against the whole social and economic system, not merely against inequalities. The fantasy of a real revolt by significant numbers of "the poor" and "the people" had never been abandoned by the Symbionese. At the same time, Teko's credo has a valedictory sound. It is boastful enough, and maintains the assurance of earlier communications. But it speaks very much in the past tense, of deeds already accomplished.

Greetings to the People

My name is Teko. I am a white revolutionary and a soldier in the Symbionese Liberation Army. I have a message for all my white brothers who have not yet come forward to fight for the freedom of all the oppressed people.

Contrary to what many of us may think, the special privileges white men as a group have gained for themselves through the oppression of all other people has never secured for us the freedom we desire. White men must understand that they will live under the threat of death as long as they continue to oppress the members of any class or group who have the strength and determination to fight back. White men themselves have only one avenue to freedom and that is to join in fighting to the death those who are and those who aspire to be the slave masters of the world.

Many of us have been bold enough to intellectualize about revolution, but far too chickenshit to get down and help make it. Most of us have been nearly fatally stricken with the vile sickness of racism. Again, most of us have been immobilized by our sexist egos and have watched and done nothing as our sisters have rushed by us into battle. We have fooled ourselves into believing that Madison Avenue piggery will bring us eternal bourgeoise happiness. If we haven't bought into the racist, sexist, capitalist, imperialist program, we have "greened-out" in Mendocino and New Hampshire. To Black people, who lead our struggle to freedom, we have proved to be the racist punks of the world when we kick-back and live off the blood and lives of the people.

However many of us have seen through this sham, and are fighting beside comrades from all races and classes, women and men, old and young. We know we have a long way to go to purify our minds of the many bourgeoise poisons but we also know that this isn't done through bullshitting and ego tripping, it is done by fighting and, as the Comrade has taught us by stalking the pig, seizing him by the tusks and riding his pig ass into his grave. It is done by unleashing the most devastating revolutionary violence ever imagined, by proving that all races and groups of people can unite and fight together for the true freedom of us all.

When we call on the people to join us in the fight for freedom many of you wonder how you can join the Symbionese Liberation Army, feeling that joining materially with those who are already fighting will provide the security you need to justify risking your lives. But we soldiers in the SLA say to this mistaken reasoning that you must read again our declaration of Revolutionary War and Terms of Military Political Alliance. The SLA came into being because many people refused to wait for so-called revolutionary groups and organizations to lead them into a revolution which would, therefore, never come. We grew tired of waiting for mythological North American revolutionaries with the necessary expertise and skills we lacked to teach us.

We have learned much from many brave revolutionary women and men, but in reality we are fighting today because we ourselves have seized the moment, taught ourselves, developed incredible strength, determination and committed ourselves to never compromise with the enemy. As anyone with the most primitive of revolutionary mentalities knows, the people will not be given their freedom, they will have to seize it. Wait for no one my brothers.

DEATH TO THE FASCIST INSECT THAT PREYS UPON THE LIFE
OF THE PEOPLE

SCREED TWENTY FIVE

A NOTE ON MEDIA AND MESSAGE

Following Teko, an unknown young woman read a screed chiefly concerned with designs of "the enemy" to suppress SLA documents. Like Teko, this person struck a valedictory note, not quite saying goodbye but clearly hinting that some profound change in the SLA operational system had begun to take place. The belief of the SLA screed-writers that perusal of their screeds would actually lead people to revolt was once more enunciated. This soldierly reference to the enemy killing its own kind applies to the hypothesis well known in race circles, that the worst of race-related crimes are organized as deliberate provocation by whites or by the police. The more local application, which had then been in circulation a full month, envisaged the murder of Miss Hearst by the police or FBI with the approval of her own family.

Up until now, the fascist media has [sic] printed our documents in full because of their vested interest in Patricia From now on however, since this pressure point no longer exists, the fascist corporate military state, via the media, will lie about and distort any information concerning the SLA

They will do this (1) in retaliation for being put in a position I that required them to print everything (2) to try to isolate us from the people, and (3) to discourage the people from joining the forces Therefore, the people must watch and listen with keen perception We will speak to you through action Analyze these actions carefully, making sure to recognize when the ENEMY is in the disguise of revolutionaries They will do anything to stop the rising of the people, including killing their own kind and blaming the people's forces under the pretense of a race war.

Remember that the SLA was born from the spirit of the people. The SLA is the PEOPLE'S ARMY, and we fight in their interests. The SLA will never compromise. The SLA will not allow the enemy jive [ie, lies] to deceive us into passively accepting genocide.

LISTEN AND WATCH, and let that spirit become your name.

SCREED TWENTY SIX

FAHIZAH AND THE FIFTH PROPHET

Walking openly in the San Francisco streets, Fahizah had dispatched the bouquet of roses and the jocular screed of April 1. Still operating with boldness and independence, she wrote the most extraordinary of the new screeds of April 4.

Bolstered by her Christian upbringing and by a literary education, she was then able to offer Field Marshal Cinque as a qualified folk-hero or savior, one who comes from nowhere, fights to free his people, and passes into the shadows with a promise to return, a new Elijah, Arthur, or Jesse James, if not a new Christ. Her statement that "Cinque" means "fifth prophet" has no lexicographical support, but provides her with opportunity to present the SLA leader as the legitimate successor to celebrated Blacks of the recent past.

As in her first long contribution (Screed 10), Fahizah insists upon the spiritual and artistic qualities of the SLA movement. Her best artist is her own leader, necessarily, since, as she says, "We have begun to redefine art as the natural creative reflection of our desperate struggle to survive. As an atheist and Marxist materialist, Fahizah also carefully redefined the spirit and all that is called spiritual". In its emphasis on sacrifice, on love, and on the transcendental part of dialectics, Fahizah's new gospel effectively introduced the emotional sweetness of Cinque's own farewell, which followed immediately on the tape and typescript.

Love to our sisters and brothers in prisons; courage & [sic] faith to our two captured soldiers; greetings to all oppressed peoples; may we connect. My name is Fahizah.

The SLA is taking these opportunities to speak with the people now, because we have been having a temporary period of inactivity while waiting for the completion of our unit's last action. We know that the people want far more than 6 million dollars of food; & we will continue to fight for the total liberation of all oppressed peoples by the only means available, that is force of arms. The Court of the People has issued The Codes of War of the Symbionese Liberation Army and I wish to state that Cinque Mtume is the General Field Marshal of the Symbionese Guerilla Forces, as well as chairman of the United Symbionese War Council. Cinque is a black brother who spent many years of his life in fascist Amerika's concentration camps: manchild years in prison cells & many years in prison cells. Cinque met literally thousands of black, brown, red, yellow & white freedom fighters while he was locked down, courageous comrade George Jackson was one among them. The spirit of all the brothers Cinque knows lives in him now, and the spirit of all the sisters that Cinque never had the opportunity to meet, but knows by common bond like Assata Shakur, Lolita Lebron & Bernadine Dohrn is always in his heart.

When Cinque escaped alone on foot from Soledad prison he did so for one reason only: TO FIGHT WITH THE PEOPLE & TO LEAD THE PEO-PLE IN REVOLUTION. He did not escape so that he could kick-back & hide & get high: he did not even escape so that he could satisfy a deep and longing personal ache to simply see the people, and be on the streets and re-unite with his family and be a father once again to his children. Cinque escaped so that he could actively stalk the fascist insect that preys upon the life of the people. The lives both he & the people's fighting forces lead now may be harsh and dangerous, but it is better to work with hard reality, than to play in pleasant, but unproductive, enslaving dreams.

Cinque Mtume is the name that was bestowed upon him by 1st his imprisoned sisters & brothers. It is the name of an ancient African Chief who led the fight of his people for freedom The name means Fifth Prophet, and Cin (Cinque) was many years ago given this name because of his keen instinct and senses, his spiritual consciousness and his deep love for all the people and children of this earth This does not, however mean that Cinque is from God or someone that is holy or that he has an extreme ego problem, but simply that he to us and to all oppressed peoples is the instilled hope and spirit of his people & all peoples and that he is of the~ people and from the people A prophet is a leader and fighter who is one of the people Leaders are individuals who within themselves feel that it is time to lead and bring us one step closer to freedom for all peoples A leader is one who is able to sense and to see what is coming at us. A leader is one who is able to help the' people understand the swiftness and fierceness with which they must move if they would survive.

Part of the revolutionary process in which we are engaged involves the constant redefining of thought, word, and action We must deal with all the conditions outside ourselves which oppress and enslave us, and we must deal with the enemy within; we must deal with both these diseases simultaneously, and with an unrelenting commitment and understanding that in reality we are not living to die, but rather all who chose to fight to the death are dying to live Cin's example to the people has taught us thru his actions and by his own words, that he or she who is scared and seeks to run from death will find it, but she or he who is NOT AFRAID and who actively seeks death out will find it NOT AT THEIR DOOR.

We embrace the concepts of art and spiritual consciousness in material relevant terms based upon the common conditions of all oppressed peoples We have begun to redefine art as the natural creative reflection of our desperate struggle to survive. Art for us is the total process of sharing and communally using what we learn in order to live and to fight. We recognize Cin as an artist for what he teaches the people, but we also realize as he himself has said, that truth has no author. Another thing which we feel is necessary to clarify is the word spirit & all that which is called spiritual. The spirit is the bodies and souls of all the people, and the spiritual is the intensity of our common instincts, as reflected thru out history to fight for the freedom of all oppressed peoples, to save the earth and the children from the putrid disease of bourgeois mentality and the putrid disease of the corporate fascist military state. In a profound and spiritual sense, as our sisters and brothers in the SLA have said, resistance to this disease is the single greatest human endeavor today.

Comrades in struggle, there is a high price that we have paid and will pay for our mistakes, and there is an even higher price which we have been paying for the loss of our leaders. We are speaking to the people now, because we all know that we cannot afford the loss of another leader; and we want the people to know that in spite of the enemy's technology and prestige of terror we DO have a leader that loves the people, and lives and fights for the people. This example helps to make a love among comrades that gives attention, appreciation, care and protection from each brother and sister to the other.

The oppressed peoples of this nation have and will continue to bring forth their leaders, prophets & fighters until they are free. The people brought forth Malcolm X who came to unite the people and warn the enemy of what would inevitably happen if the people were not freed. The enemy answered by murdering Malcolm. The people then did again bring forth another prophet, that prophet was Martin Luther King who with non-violence & humanity pleaded to the enemy to free the people. And just when King was ready to declare that nonviolent protest would accomplish nothing but the further enslavement and degradation of the people, the enemy murdered King. George Jackson was a prophet & leader from the streets & when the enemy imprisoned him, George received his education in the raw; he learned firsthand that there can be NO compromise with merciless pigs. George Jackson came from the prisons of Amerikkka & love-inspired he boldly fought the oppressor. When the fascist insect locked him down and murdered him, the people knew that they had suffered'. a great loss, but they failed to unite in immediate retaliation. Now, once again, the people have brought forth another prophet and leader.

This leader comes not to beg and plead with the enemy, he comes not to warn of violence, but is himself the bringer of the children of the wind and the SOUND OF WAR. He has ONE WORD to the children of the oppressed and the children of the oppressor: COME. We have joined together with love and unity and the understanding that those who would be free, must themselves STRIKE THE FIRST BLOW.

Screed Twenty Seven

CINQUE'S FAREWELL

The typescript provided by the SLA to prevent error in the transcription of their tape may have been made partly from a stenographic pickup of an ad-lib pronouncement Cinque's voice on the tape was as easy, bold and eloquent as ever but had a new richness to it and ended with a new sweetness. Like the other speakers, but with greater authority, he, shadowed forth an oncoming change in the affairs of the SLA First for the SLA then for himself he shut the door on the Hearst operation.

The three enemies of the people now sentenced to death had earned that destiny in disparate ways. All were old friends and co-workers of key people of the SLA. Robin Steiner, a Florida girl, had come to Berkeley with Russell Little and been on the fringes of Telegraph Avenue revolutionism before the SLA went underground. That she had informed to the FBI was publicly denied by her Florida lawyer Little himself; in a message sent to the media from his jail cell said that the sentence of death was an error. Chris Thompson, a quiet-voiced Black militant of Berkeley, had sold a pistol to Uttle for use in SLA work, but was not himself in the organization. His crime was giving testimony to the grand jury which indicted Remiro and Little Colston Westbrook, a Black teacher in Berkeley, had been one of the pioneers in the development of Black Cultural programs in California prisons. As the Black Cultural Association moved towards theories of terror, he had drawn away. But he had remained in close contact with East Bay revolutionists of all persuasions, and had recently elected to provide information to the police.

Of more interest than these casual sentences of death are Cinque's disposition of the Little-Remiro problem and the Hearst problem. The release of Little and Remiro, in exchange for the release of Patricia Hearst, had been hinted at in screed after screed, but never actually proposed or demanded. By the beginning of April, the SLA leaders had determined that such an exchange was not in the cards at all. Cinque now offered a kind farewell to his captive soldiers. Avenged they might be, exchanged they would not be. Cinque's ukase on their destiny exactly fitted his ukase on the destiny of Miss Hearst. His announcement of this strange destiny brought fear, consternation, and perhaps contrition to the Hearsts, the contending groups and agencies of the PIN fiasco, and many of the people who, one by one, had bubbled to the surface in media and before the public.

[I]

This is Field Marshall [sic on all slips] Cin.

I would like to take this opportunity on behalf of the Federation to thank WAPAC and all the coalition members for their aid in feeding and educating the people; we send you our faith and unity to always serve the people.

[II]

I wish to say to those who speak about what they want, to you I say that your words and cries will bring you nothing but a wet face and an empty heart, the enemy is unhearing and he is unmerciful to the oppressed. If you would have freedom for your children, then you as all oppressed people will have to fight and struggle for it. Freedom is not tax deductible, nor is it willed to you, no piece of paper can sign it over to you or your children, it is something that in an oppressive world can only be gained and protected by the force of your arms and your spirit to defend that freedom at any cost.

[III]

To the people and combat forces of the people, business of the revolution: The following are enemies of the people, they are agents of the enemy and have been found guilty of working and informing to the enemy against the people, and therefore death warrants have been issued by this court against them and they should be shot on sight by any of the peoples' forces when found.

Robin Steiner: female, white age 20 hazel eyes, brown hair, 5-4, wears contact , lenses, 115 pounds, past resident of Berkeley' now living in Flonda an informer to the FBI.

Chris Thompson: male, black, age 35, brown eyes, black hair,'6-3, Berkeley resident, is a government agent, paid informer for the FBI.

Colson Westbrook: male black, age 35 brown eyes, brown hair, 5-8, 210 pounds, Berkeley language instructor, resident of Oakland, is a government agent worked for CIA in Vietnam as interrogator and torturer in the Phoenix operation, and also served same purposes in other foreign countries, now working for military intelligence while giving cross assistance to the FBI.

These subjects are to be shot on sight wherever found and at any time.

[IV]

Concerning the Hearst operation:

The government dictatorship as well as the Hearst Empire has shown that they are quite willing to murder even their own to maintain power over the people, therefore it is the judgment of this court that in future NO prisoners of the ruling class or its executive agents will be taken prisoner. The Court of the People this date issues the following order: All corporate enemies of the people will be SHOT on sight at any time and at any place. This order is permanent, until such time as all enemy forces have either surrendered or been destroyed.

Concerning the protective custody prisoner: The subject has been freed but has refused to go home or take part as a member of the enemy fascist state. There is no further need to discuss the release of the prisoner under this condition since the prisoner is now a comrade and has been accepted into the ranks of the people's army as a comrade and fighter for the people's freedom. And therefore there is no further basis for negotiations since subject may leave whenever she feels that she wishes to do so. She is armed and well capable to defend herself. This operation is hereby terminated and suspension of offensive operations is hereby rescinded and all combat forces of the SLA and all people's forces are requested and so ordered to resume normal offensive combat operations against all enemies of the people. The Court of the People wishes to note that the people DO NOT wish to be fed by the rich, the people want back the land.

To our two soldiers who are in the hands of the enemy and to all our comrades behind the walls: As you know we have learned a hard lesson from our mistakes, and will learn from this for the future and the war that we the people will win. I am sure that you understand that under our codes of war there can be no surrender to the enemy, at any time or at any price. You both have shown correct actions in recognizing that even though you are innocent of any crimes it is not possible for you to receive a fair trial in the enemy's arena. I deeply regret that you were not offensively prepared to attack rather than be seized by the enemy. I send you my love, and the love of all of your comrades, and courage in your determination to carry on the struggle even from that side of the wall, as we will NEVER relent from this end. In this way we do expect to meet again.

[V]

I would like to take this opportunity to speak to my six lovely black babies. Victor, Damon, Sherry, Sherlyne, Dawn and Dede, I want you to know that to just say your names again fills my heart with joy. I want you to know that I love you all with all the love that a father can have for those so dear to him; and I want you to understand also that I have not forgotten my promise to you, that whenever you needed me, I would be there at your side, and so, I am now even when you may not see me, I am there; because no matter where I am, I am fighting for your freedom, your future and your life. Daddy wants you to understand that I can't come home because you and the people are not free and as long as the enemy exists I can find no rest nor any hope for you or our people as a whole. I can't be happy when the enemy murders the children of other fathers and mothers. I want you to understand that I have to fight for you and for all fathers and mothers who must stay home, or who have not the courage to fight or the clear understanding yet, that the greatest gift they give their children is FREEDOM.

So, to you my children, even when I may never see you again, know that I love you and will not for any price forsake your freedom and the freedom of all oppressed peoples. To you I give all that a father could wish, I give you life without fear exploitation, I give you love with a future and understanding t the price of freedom is daring to struggle, daring to win. In ending this letter to you, I ask only one thing of you all, that is promise me that you will always honor the people and love the children and defend them both at any price against the enemy.

In closing I will play the national anthem of the Symbionese Liberation Army: My people, my brothers, my sisters FREE THE PEOPLE. FREE THE LAND. AND SAVE THE CHILDREN

[The anthem was a rock-music radio tune picked up, and replayed, via the SLA tape recorder.]

SCREED TWENTY EIGHT

PATRICIA HEARST

Patricia Hearst brought the Symbionese story full circle by citing, as~ the prime proof of fascism and tyranny, the long-forgotten death of the Oakland youth Tyrone Guyton. More wildly than the SLA people ~ themselves she predicted a national breakdown ~a state of total unemployment and a government program of mass deportation and geno-cide She blamed her parents for cruelty and falsehood not only to "the people" and "the poor," but to herself, and for the last time blamed the FBI and the fascist corporate state for seeking to kill her.

The communication brought forth a storm of new speculation, and~ many an expert, amateur or professional,, was able to spread his theories for the day allotted to him. It was argued that Patricia Hearst was truly in the SLA, or that she was in it after being brainwashed, or that she had read the message, and half made it up, in fear for her life. And that she was alive now, somewhere, in or out of the SLA, or else that she was dead.

Hearst-case reportage continued, for new crimes and new poses continued to spin off from the central act. But the great main story had passed into absurdity and begun its swift descent.

[I]

To those who would bear the hopes and future of our people, let the voice of their guns express the words of freedom.

I would like to begin this statement by informing the public that I wrote what I am about to say. It's what I feel. I have never been forced to say any-thing on any tape. Nor have I been brainwashed, drugged, tortured, hypno-tized or in any way confused. As George Jackson wrote, "It's me, the way I want it, the way I see it."

[II]

Mom, Dad, I would like to comment on your efforts to supposedly secure my safety. The PIN giveaway was a sham. You attempted to deceive the people. You were playing games, stalling for time - time which the FBI was using in their [sic on all slips] attempts to assassinate me and the SLA elements. You continued to report that you did everything in your power to pave the way for negotiations for my release -- I hate to believe that you could have been so unimaginative as not to have even considered getting Little and Remiro released on bail.

While it was repeatedly stated that my conditions would at all times correspond with those of the captured soldiers, when your own lawyer went to inspect the "hole" at San Quentin, he approved the deplorable conditions there another move which potentially jeopardized my safety. My mother's acceptance of the appointment to a second term as a U.C. regent, as you well knew, would have caused my immediate execution had the SLA been less than "together" about their political goals. Your actions have taught me a great lesson, and in a strange kind of way, I'm grateful to you.

Steven [Steven Weed], I know that you are beginning to realize that there is no such thing as neutrality in time of war. There can be no compromise as your experience with the FBI must have shown you. You have been harassed by the FBI because of your supposed connections with so-called radicals, and some people have even gone so far as to suggest that I arranged my own arrest. We both know what really came down that Monday night [February 4, when she was kidnapped] but you don't know what's happened since then. I have changed, grown. I've become conscious and can never go back to the life we led before. What I'm saying may seem cold to you and to my old friends, but love doesn't mean the same thing to me anymore. My love has expanded as a result of my experiences to embrace all people. It's grown into an unselfish love for my comrades here, in prison and on the streets. A love that comes from the knowledge that one is free until we are all free. While I wish that you could be comrade, I don't expect it all, I expect is that you try I understand the changes I've gone through

[III]

I have been given the choice of (one) being released in a safe area, or (two), joining the forces of the Symbionese Liberation Army and fighting for my freedom and the freedom of all oppressed people. I have chosen to stay and fight. One thing which I have learned is that the corporate ruling class will do anything in their power in order to maintain their position of control over th masses, even if this means the sacrifice of one of their own. I should be obvious that people who don't even care about the own children couldn't possibly care about anyone else's children~ The things which are precious to these people are their money and power, and they will never willingly surrender either People should not have to humiliate themselves by standing in line in order to be fed, nor should they have to live in fear of their lives and the lives of their children, as Tyrone Guyton's mother will sadly attest to.

Dad, you said that you were concerned with my life, and you also said that you were concerned with the life and interests of all oppressed people in this country, but you are a liar in both areas and as a member of the ruling class, I know for sure that yours and Mom's interests are never the interests of the people. Dad, you said you would see about getting more job opportunities for the people, but why haven't you warned the people what is going to happen to them, that actually the few jobs they still have will be taken away.

You, a corporate liar, of course will say that you don't know what I am talking about, but I ask you then to prove it, tell the poor and oppressed people of this nation what the corporate state is about to do, warn black and poor people that they are about to be murdered down to the last man, woman and child. If you're so interested in the people why don't you tell them what the energy crisis really is. Tell them how it's nothing more than a manufactured strategy, a way of hiding industry's real intentions. Tell the people that the energy crisis is nothing more than a means to get public approval for a massive program to build nuclear power plants all over the nation.

Tell the people that the entire corporate state is, with the aid of this massive power supply, about to totally automate the entire industrial state, to the point that in the next five years all that will be needed will be a small class of button pushers, tell the people, Dad, that all of the lower class and at least half of the middle class will be unemployed in the next three years, and that the removal of expendable excess, the removal of unneeded people has already started. I want you to tell the people the truth. Tell them how the law and order programs are just a means to remove so-called violent (meaning aware) individuals from the community in order to facilitate the controlled removal of unneeded labor forces from this country, in the same way that Hitler controlled the removal of the Jews from Germany.

I should have known that if you and the rest of the corporate state were willing to do this to millions of people to maintain power and to serve your needs, you would also kill me if necessary to serve those same needs. How long will it take before white people in this country understand that whatever happens to a black child happens sooner or later to a white child. How long will it be before we all understand that we must fight for our freedom?

[IV]

I have been given the name Tania after a comrade who fought alongside Che

(Guevara) in Bolivia for the people of Bolivia. I embrace the name with the determination to continue fighting with her spirit. There is no victory in half-assed attempts at revolution. I know Tania dedicated her life to the people. Fighting with total dedication and an intense desire to learn, which I will continue in the oppressed American people's revolution. All colors of string in the web of humanity yearn for freedom!

Osceola [Russell Little] and Bo [Joseph Remiro], even though we have never met I feel like I know you. Timing brought me to you and I'm fighting with your freedom and the freedom of all prisoners in mind. In the strenuous jogs that life takes, you are pillars of strength to me. If I'm feeling down, I think of you, of where you are and why you are there, and my determination grows stronger. It's good to see that your spirits are so high in-spite of the terrible conditions.

Even though you aren't here, you are with other strong comrades, and the three of us are learning. Together, I, in an environment of love and you in one of hate, in the belly of the fascist beast. We have grown closer to the people and become stronger through our experiences. I have learned how vicious the pig really is, and our comrades are teaching me to attack with even greater viciousness, in the knowledge that the people will win. I send greetings, to Death Row Jeff, Al Taylor and Raymond Scott [all convicts]. Your concern for my safety is matched by my concern for yours. We share a common goal as revolutionaries knowing that Comrade George lives.

It is in the spirit of Tania that I say, "PATRIA O MUERTE. VENCERE-MOS".

SCREED TWENTY NINE

CINQUE ON COBRA AND ZEBRA

After the message of April's Fool's Day, the SLA was silent for two weeks. Exhausted by their ordeal and dismayed by Patricia's metamorphosis into Tania, the Hearsts slipped off to Mexico. From a vacation villa in that warm nation, Randolph Hearst complained that the SLA had not played fair with him, and that he was disillusioned about their "good intentions". Similarly inadequate comments came from Weed, Kramer, the Berkeley revolutionaries, and others. The free-food program was terminated in Fresno just as it had begun in Oakland, namely with a riot, injuries, and arrests. Media stardoms shifted a little, moving from Black actionists, who now drew back, to professors and psychologists who eagerly replaced them.

While the police and FBI maintained a grim silence, a few enterprising reporters turned up the basic data on the SLA membership. As it now appeared, all but two, or possibly one, of the SLA people were college-educated Telegraph Avenue whites. All were ordinary Berkeley revolutionists, trite veterans of movements to "green" the nation and to "liberate" women, homosexuals, poets, South Vietnamese, Angolans, Catholic Irish, and children, as well as prisoners. Except for Cinque, their captive Black leader, they were all in their twenties. They had prepared their programs with great care, and done a great deal of practice shooting in basements and rifle ranges. To most of the other revolutionary spirits of Berkeley and Oakland they had seemed dangerous and counter-productive, especially after the murder of Marcus Foster. But from motives of loyalty, existential non-involvement, and sheer trembling cowardice, these other revolutionists had maintained silence about them and their plans.

Even as the names and histories of the SLA soldiers came out the newer set of "Zebra" crimes began to occupy the headlines. This was a new program of so-called "senseless slayings" or "random murders" of whites by Blacks on the streets of San Francisco and other cities. Shootings in this racially specialized series now totalled eighteen, and twelve of the San Francisco victims had been killed outright. The San Francisco Police Department, which had already mounted a massive program to stop these killings, now adopted the technique of accosting and questioning young Blacks who answered descriptions of the killers. There was an immediate protest from Black politicians and other race leaders. Court injunctions, "emergency meetings", riotous protests staged for the camera, and all the rest of the race-politics paraphernalia now filled the media. Quite by accident, the series of Black-white murders had acquired its poetic code-name Zebra. While the SLA lay quiet, their animal, the Cobra, slipped to the back pages, while the Zebra of the bloodier new episode dominated the emotions of the Bay Area peoples.

The next move of the SLA, namely the robbery of a San Francisco bank, took place after this shift of racial attention from Cobra to Zebra. Selected for attack was the Sunset branch of the Hibernia Bank, a quiet establishment in a quiet neighborhood. Into the bank at 10:30 AM on April 15, stormed Field Marshal Cinque and a little army of heavily armed white women. These included Patricia "Mizmoon" Soltysic, Soltysic's lesbian lover Camilla Hall, the lyric screedsperson Fahizah, and Patricia or Tania Hearst. Outside, the four or five other members of the Liberation Army manipulated four rented cars in an escape system. Security cameras in the bank photographed the whole scene. The operation went off flawlessly, or would have, except that at the very end Cinque gratuitously shot down two elderly bystanders.

Screed 28, with the two which followed it, was read onto tape, packaged in tinfoil, and addressed to the still-favored WAPAC. By some slip or change in the plans, it went to an anonymous Black citizen, from him to another, and from the other to a Black police inspector, and so to the media and the FBI. In this screed, Cinque misrepresented the wanton shooting of the bystanders, pedantically enumerated weaponry used and weaponry "liberated" (from the bank guard), and introduced a new Symbionese calender system through which 1974 became "the year of the soldier". Of much more significance, Cinque attempted to regain the attention of the Bay Area Black communities by wedding his Cobra to the maturing Zebra. According to him, the casual butchery of the Zebra slayings must be thought of as a police gambit, the immediate purpose of which was "to entrap the SLA forces and more precisely to assassinate myself", and the general purpose of which was "to commit a race war" and "to remove young blacks from the community".

Other comments of Cinque in this screed reflect other events with which the SLA wished to connect itself. In particular, his plaint about the "disarming" of "the people" refers to another Berkeley-Oakland incident Following an assault complaint East Bay policemen had entered a Black Muslim barracks and confiscated an enormous arsenal of firearms, plus some narcotics and stolen property. Black counter-action, which took the usual form of civil-rights lawsuits and televised screams about harassment and genocide, had represented another threat to the SLA domination of the media.

[I]

To those who would bear the hopes and future of our people, let the voice of their guns express their wills of freedom.
Greetings to the people and all sisters and brothers behind the, walls and in the streets. To elements of the Black Liberation Army,) the Weather Underground and the Black Guerrilla Family, and all combat forces of the community.

I am General Field Marshall Cin speaking.

[II]

Combat operations: April 15, the year of the soldier.
Action: Appropriation.
Supplies liberated: One .38 Smith and Wesson revolver, condition good. Five rounds of 158 grain .30 caliber ammo. Cash: $10,660,02.
Number of rounds fired by combat forces: Seven rounds.
Number of rounds lost: Five.
Casualities: People's forces, none. Enemy forces, none. Civilian, two.

Reasons: Subject One, Male. Subject was ordered to lay [sic] on the floor face down. Subject refused order and jumped out the front door of the bank. Therefore the subject was shot. Subject Two, Male. Subject failed or did not hear warning to clear the street. Subject was running down the street toward the bank, and combat forces accordingly assumed subject was an armed enemy force element. Therefore the subject was shot.

We again warn the public. Any citizen attempting to aid, to inform, or to assist the enemy of the people in any manner will be shot without hesitation. There is no middle ground in war. Either you are the people of the enemy. You must make the choice.

[III]

As a Black man and a father and as a representative of Black people, I would like to say that I, as well as many other Black people, have been watching the actions taken against Black people within the city of San Francisco, and also in Berkeley and Oakland, by the racist agents of the ruling class.

Like most of my people, I never trust anything the enemy says or does. I must at all times be suspicious or distrust any acts on his part as not being what they first seem to be. Following this principle, I must look at the so-called Zebra operation with more attention, since it is an action against the freedom of the people.

For the love that I hold for the people drives myself and all the SLA to understand that we must fight and defend the people.

I at first had thought that Operation Zebra was really nothing more than a normal counter-insurgency operation to attempt to entrap the SLA forces, and more precisely to assassinate myself. I say assassinate because the enemy knows by now who I am, and [tape blurred: that I will not fail the people? J that I represent as long as I am alive.

He understands that if he can terrorize and disarm the Black community with some action adjoining me, then he will be able to isolate me specifically and to kill me, thereby not allowing me the time to educate [tape blurred: the people and children?] of the community to become leaders of our people. He also understands that I have been bringing the children of the oppressed and the children of the oppressor together. He understands that I am bringing the truth to the children and opening their eyes to the real enemy of humanity by simply allowing them to see the enemy as he truly is, and allowing them to find out really who the people are; and that the [we?] people love them and will welcome them with open arms if they will just come.

In short, he knows that the SLA is building an army of the people. That is the army which by its very composition can truly destroy the enemy and free the people.

[IV]

At this time I am more inclined to feel, however, that Operation Zebra is a lot more than just entrapping the SLA. In fact I feel the enemy knows that he or she can never totally entrap all the SLA forces regardless of the size of the city in which counterinsurgency operations may take place. The [tape blurred: enemy's false pretenses?] that the SLA are under surveillance by the FBI is designed to demoralize the people and attempt to make them believe in the prestige of the enemy.

In any event, once understanding these points we come back again to the same question: What is Operation Zebra? If Operation Zebra is not merely a counter-insurgency operation, then what is it9 And if we look closely we begin to see the truth that Operation Zebra is a planned enemy offensive against the people to commit a race war. This could possibly be the only way the enemy can stop the SLA from bringing all oppressed people together against the common enemy.

Operation Zebra is even more than that. The so-called Zebra killer will never be found, because it is the only justification, notwithstanding [sic] martial law being declared, whereby the enemy can stop and arrest any Black male. In fact we can expect in the next few months, under the guise of searching for the so-called Zebra killer, block by block and house by house searches. And of course all weapons found in the people's homes will be confiscated under the guise of stolen property or that [sic] they have to be verified as not being the murder weapon. In short, the people will be disarmed.

Operation Zebra shows up even another purpose of the enemy. It is a means to remove as many Black males from the community as possible, at the same time pressing all Black males to submit to FBI classification and identification, which is being applied in the form of so-called police passes, by using each person's driver's license or Social Security card numbers, which are, I may mention, pre-codes for the FBI computer systems.

[V]

Now people, I warn you again: The only way, I repeat, the only way you will regain your life and freedom is to fight.

The only way you can keep your guns is to use them.
Your time is running short. Open your eyes.

Death to the Fascist insect that preys upon the life of the people.

SCREED THIRTY

TEKO ON COBRA AND ZEBRA

From one point of view Cinque was only a token Black in an all-white enterprise. To disguise its minimal Negritude, the SLA had earlier adopted a play-school tactic of "let's pretend". Following this tactic, several of the former tape-makers had tried to disguise their middle-class collegiate white voices under heavy Black American accents. Thus spoke Teko. (Bill Harris) Teko had by now been thoroughly identified. Besides being an imitation poor Black, he was a prosperous white, a BA and MA of Indiana University, and an ex-teacher. He and his wife, also prosperous, college-trained, and a teacher, were the only married couple in the SLA. In a dialect much more Negroid than Cinque's own, Teko continued Cinque's line about race war and genocide, and contemplated what he called "the rising tide of Black revolution". Like Cinque too, he demanded for Cobra the media attention which was shifting towards Zebra.

Greetings to the people. This is Teko speaking.

As it has been stated many times by the Black community, the Zebra operation is a planned enemy offensive against the people to create a race war. Race war is a fascist tactic to divide the people. The pigs know that there is no [other?] way to control or eliminate the people's army.

The people's army in the United States of America means a guerrilla force of Black, brown, red, yellow, and white people united by their fighting spirit and a common determination to kill the pig. The Symbionese Liberation Army is a people's army and the only way the fascists can slow us down is to try to scare the people into fighting among themselves.

The pigs and the fascist media have by their slick trickery attempted to link the SLA with the so-called Zebra killings. They have even gone so far as to release a composite drawing and description of the killer which has a resemblance to General Field Marshal Cinque. [A blurred phrase.) The next lie that we expect t hear is that Cinque is the Zebra killer, and this will be even pig justification to continue the harassment and disarming of people.

The pigs hope to manipulate the fear and racism of the broad mass of unconscious whites in order to eliminate black revolutionaries. By black revolutionaries we mean Black people in general. Pigs like Alioto wish to maneuver these white people into allowing the fascist army to sweep the ghettos and machine-gun and imprison the people. But anyone who by their racism and government-manipulated fear supports genocide makes the glaring error of forging his or her own slave chains. And if white people in fascist America don't think they are enslaved they only prove their own foolishness.

The enemy has kept us divided for hundreds of years and for at least that long the pig has made uncountable attempts at eliminating the rising tide of Black revolution. But Black people, by their strength and determination, have survived this fascist onslaught. Black people, more revolutionary than ever before, are armed and angry.

And now the SLA is proving that Black people's ain't alone, that the thing the pigs hate and fear the most is happening, is growing The people's army [is] of irate niggers of all races, including whites, not talkers but fighters. The enemy recognizes that the people are on the brink of revolution, and the enemy will do anything at any cost to prevent this.

We ask the people, especially whites, to carefully analyze Operation Zebra. The Black [tape and faked accent very blurred) with the times, and to understand who in reality sits in the saddle and holds the reins.

Death to the fascist insect that preys upon the life of the people.

SCREED THIRTY ONE

TAN1A HEARST

Before the bank robbery, many pundits and specialists had offered opinions to the effect that Miss Hearst could not have become a "sincere" member of the SLA. In the days immediately after the robbery, it was urged that she had entered the bank drugged, had entered it with her hands tied to an empty carbine, or had entered it under the ready guns of her SLA manipulators. By snarling out such commands as "Get down, or I'll blow your motherfucking heads off", Tania had seemed to take a stand even during the robbery. In her part of the post-robbery tape, she attempted to put the question permanently to rest.

Not only the Hearsts, Weed, and other intimates, but also a host of outsiders, had gotten into the media by asking that Miss Hearst come in person, alone, to explain whether she was still a prisoner, or truly a member of the SLA. The new Tania now rejected all such appeals. The cruel language of her rejection reflects her new association with the Berkeley street people. But it remained difficult for people sensitive to language to believe that she could have gotten the Lib crudities of pig and ageist and Adolf into her communicative system in so short a time.

Though Miss Hearst's voice on the tape was clear and strong, the situation it revealed did not inspire confidence. Many mature watchers of the SLA speculated that her life was more endangered now than ever before. By taking part in the bank robbery the had finished the process of identifying herself with the SLA. Her death by any violent means could now be laid with better color to the machinations of the long pre-accused FBI.

Greetings to the people. This is Tania.

On April 15, my comrades and I expropriated $ 10,660.02 from the Sunset branch of the Hibernia Bank. Casualties could have been avoided had the persons involved kept out of the way, and cooperated with the people's forces until after our departure.

I was positioned so that I could hold down customers and bank personnel who were on the floor. My gun was loaded, and at no time did any of my comrades intentionally point their guns at me. Careful examination of the photographs which were published clearly shows that this was true.

Our action of April 15 forced the corporate fascist state to help finance the revolution. In the case of expropriation, the difference between a criminal act and a revolutionary act is shown by what the money is used for.

As for [ie, just as?] the money involved in my parents' bad faith gesture to aid the people, these funds are being used to aid the people and to insure the survival of the people's forces in their struggle with, and for, the people.

To the clowns who want a personal interview with me, Vincent Hallinan, Steven Weed, and the Pig Hearsts:

I prefer giving it to the people in the bank. It is absurd to think that I could surface to say what am I saying now, and still be allowed to freely return to my comrades The enemy still wants me dead.

I am obviously alive and well As for being brainwashed, the idea is ridiculous to the point of being beyond belief It is interesting the way earlier reports characterized me as a beautiful, intelligent liberal, while in more recent reports I am a common girl who has been brainwashed The contradictions are obvious.

Consciousness is terrifying to the ruling class; and they will do anything to discredit people who have realized that the only alternative to freedom is death; and that the only way we can free ourselves of this fascist dictatorship is by fighting, not with words but with guns.

As for my ex-fiance, I am amazed that he thinks that the first thing I would want to do, once freed [sic], would be to rush and see him. I don't care if I never see him again.

During the last few months, Steven has shown himself to be a sexist, ageist [ie, age prejudiced] pig Not that this is a sudden change from the way he always was. It merely became more blatant during the period when I was still a hostage.

Frankly, Steven is the one who sounds brainwashed I can't believe that those weird words [presumably his comments on the brainwashing theory] were from his heart They were a mixture of FBI rhetoric and Randy's [ie, her father's] simplicity.

I have no proof that Mr. DeBray's letter [about an interview] is authentic. The date and location he gave were confusing in terms of when the letter was published in the papers. How could it have been written in Paris and published in your newspapers on the same day, Adolf?

In any case, I hope that the last action[at the bank] has put his mind at ease. If it did not, further actions will.

To those people who still believe that I am brainwashed or dead, I see no reason to further defend my position. I am a good soldier in the people's army.

Patria o muerte! Venceremos!

SCREED THIRTY TWO

WRITING ON THE WALLS

On Friday and Saturday, May 3 and 4, most of the media attention seemed destined to go to the Zebra killings. These were now established as the work of a cult of young Blacks calling themselves "Death Angels" and having some indistinct relationship to the Nation of Islam or so-called Black Muslims. In a daring news conference Mayor Alioto of San Francisco alleged that the fourteen previously-identified San Francisco racial shootings were part of a series of nearly eighty recent Black-white murders, mostly in Berkeley, Oakland, and San Francisco, but spilling into other parts of the state. Several cult-killer suspects were arrested and the expectable outburst of anti-police protests and civil-rights lawsuits instantly broke out.

The SLA response had been organized a week earlier, when a fragment of the SLA moved out of their small apartment at 1827 Golden Gate Avenue, in the Western Addition or WAPAC area of San Francisco. The apartment had been rented in mid-March by a white girl who gave her name as Louise Hamilton. The small apartment house, the street, and the surrounding neighborhood were all racially mixed, so that neighbors paid no attention when a Black man moved in with her.

Ultimately four people, that is Marshal Cinque and three of the white girls, lived there. Tania Hearst had spent at least part of April there. The fact that she had gone out alone to buy groceries seemed to prove that she was not under duress, much less in captivity.

Contrary to the injunctions of their Codes of War (Screed 23), the SLA soldiers had been terrible housekeepers. It was the cockroaches which flowed out into neighboring apartments which caused the manager to investigate and thus to discover who his tenants had been. He found the place filthy, battered, and stinking. Police and reporters alike, when they finally arrived, were amazed by the "indescribable filth" and "overpowering stench" of the little headquarters. Besides odor, dirty underclothes, junk hardware, sleeping bags, and an old bicycle, police found the bathtub full of an evil-smelling concoction of household chemicals. The apartment boasted no fireplace, and the chemicals had been used to melt away papers and letters belonging to the group. At the bottom of the tub were several keys, including the ignition key of one of the rented cars used in the bank robbery.

Noticing Hegel's remark that all the great events of history repeat themselves, Karl Marx added that their first occurrence was as tragedy, but the second only as farce. In abandoning their little headquarters, the SLA screedspeople, who now included Tania Hearst, wrote their messages in the emptily mocking style and the graffito medium generally employed by wicked little children. They had been transformed into "old news" by the rush of Bay Area events; they had created some squabbling, but no real race riots, much less revolutions; they were becoming the object, now, of laughter rather than fear or hate; they were still free, but they were intimately known by the police and by much of the public, and were facing capture and trial at any moment. Dirty, weary, nervous, bored, the world-renowned Symbionese Liberation Army was returning to the nothing it set out from.

The writings were done via felt pens on off-white painted walls. The "Charles" in

Graffito A is Charles Bates, the FBI leader who still stumbled along in charge of the case. Its author was probably Nancy Ling Perry, or Fahizah. The poem "A New Year's Resolution", doubtless the work of Camilla Hall, the SLA Sappho, takes us back past the Hearst operation to the days of attack on the Oakland schools and Oakland police. "Ho" is Ho Chi Minh, the North Korean leader in whom the radical youth of the 1960's found their hero and prophet. Cinque and Tania identify their more modest contributions. Odd obscenities and old mottoes are by no particular author. Four cobras, each with its inconvenient seven heads, writhed among the messages on the walls.

A. A Toilet Message

WARNING!
To the FBI, CIA, DIA, NSA, NBC, and CBS:
There are a few clues in this bathroom. However, you will have to wait until they are dry.
An additional word of caution: 1/2 (one-half) lb. (pound) of cyanide (potassium cyanide) crystals has been added to this "home brew." So, pig, drink at your own risk.
There are many additional juicy SLA clues throughout this safe house. However, remember that you are not bullet-proof either.
Happy hunting, Charles!

B. Miscellany

Da da, Oh my
Books, once read, make good bullet-proofing.
Death to the fascist insects that prey on the life of the people.

C. The Poem for Tyrone

A New Year's Resolution, January 1, 1974
(Dedicated to manchild Tyrone Guyton)

Is it real?
To load a gun with a magazine of dreams?
NO.
We say fire power to the people
Against the "hire" power of the ruling class.
Who chained
Hired Hands,

Feet,
And genitals.
Our grip on the gun grows stronger,
And theyyyy will no longer
See day.
They'll feel what's real
From a magazine of steel.

D. Signed Statements

Today the locust
fights the elephant.
Tomorrow the elephant
will be disembowelled.
-Ho-

Freedom is the break of the land.
-Cin-

Freedom is the will of life.
Patria o Muerte, Venceremos.
-Tania-

APPENDIX I

A GARLAND OF COUNTERSCREEDS

The written and spoken counterscreeds carried by media were enormous in number and bewildering in variety. They ran from little heartsick letters and prayers to enormously complex programmatic and exegetic discourses. They flew at one from what the SLA called "all forms of the media." They came from every intellectual stratum and every social and emotional position. There seemed no limit to what could be said about the SLA.

Counterscreed 1: THE FIRST FROM HEARST

After the kidnapping of Patricia Hearst on February 4, 1974, the Symbionese publicity staff kept its silence for over a week. In the interim many attitudes were considered by the Hearst family.

Groping in the dark, reasonably sure that the Berkeley kidnapping would have some kind of political meaning, but uncertain as to what its bearing would be, Randolph A. Hearst elected to take a soft line. The line was to become still softer in the subsequent weeks, when he knew what the SLA was, or pretended to be. Later, he and Mrs. Hearst tried to adopt the language of the Symbionese themselves, in order to placate them. When Patricia had actually turned Symbionese, he inadequately denounced these murderers and terrorists as cheaters, rip-off artists, and bad sports.

In this first response, Hearst was able to speak of the kidnapping as a crime. His statement was published in the Bay Area news media on February 6.

Mrs. Hearst and I pray to God that the men who took our daughter will show compassion and return her unharmed.

At this point, their only crime is abduction. For their sake and ours and especially for Patricia we plead with them not to make it any worse.

We do not believe we are clutching at straws when we say there is evidence that the abductors do have a measure of compassion and are not senseless and brutal.

They were heavily armed and could have eliminated all witnesses. They did not.

Neither did they harm the owner of the car they commandeered. They held him for a few hours and then released him.

In short, there are witnesses who saw the men who took our daughter. Thus, Patricia is no more a threat to them than are the others.

Doing bodily harm to her cannot help them. It can only add to the seriousness of their crime.

We want our daughter back unharmed. If she is released we will not seek to imprison her abductors.

We plead with them to communicate with us direct or through the press.

Please, we beg of you, do not compound your crime by harming our daughter.

Counterscreed 2: DAILY CAL CONTRA

One of the early rejections of the Symbionese system came from the *Daily Californian*, the powerful and generally radical student newspaper of the University of California at Berkeley. Despite some expectable backing and filling on the general theme of injustice, the Daily Cal came down hard on the SLA, and added a couple of dark hints about its having an agent-provocateur intent, or at least function, in a February 11 editorial headed "SLA TERRORISM."

The kidnapping of University student Patricia Hearst from her Berkeley apartment last week, apparently by members of the mysterious Symbionese Liberation Army, has created an atmosphere of fear throughout our community.

Much as we want to see major changes in our society, we see no way that this kidnapping can have any positive consequences. The group that claims credit for it, the SLA, has done nothing to prove that it deserves to be considered radical. They have produced no program and no strategy for change. Their only promise for the future has been a threat of further assassinations like the killing of Oakland Schools Superintendent Marcus Foster last fall, for which they claim credit along with the Hearst kidnapping.

The Berkeley community cannot accept the claim of any group of nameless individuals to carry out acts of violence in its midst.

While we do not condone the many injustices that exist in American society today, we do not see how more killings and kidnappings can do anything other than provide a springboard for police repression.

In fact, the SLA's actions provide such a convenient excuse for a police campaign against all forms of radicalism that we cannot help but wonder where their real loyalties lie. Their actions are giving all those who are really working for radical social change a bad name.

We hope the members of the Symbionese Liberation Army will release Patricia Hearst unharmed. And we strongly condemn them and any other group that brings terror into our midst.

Counterscreed 3: THE CAPTURE OF THE PRESS

The collapse of the California press before the demands of the SLA was nearly total. Curiously, however, this collapse may have assisted readers of a scholarly and reflective mind.

From the beginning of their operations, the SLA screedspeople demanded much more than ordinary vulgar publicity. Perhaps from the common and excusable vanity of authorship, perhaps from pride in themselves as political planners and constitutionalists, and certainly from vain hopes that their writings, in company with their terrorist work, would stir up a cauldron of rage and violence among Negroes and other groups of what they called "the poor and the people," they' demanded the full and complete publication of all their works, even their borrowed Cobra emblems, in "all forms of the media." Omission of any detail was regarded as an "act of bad faith" on the part of any publisher or electronic editor. During the period in which Patricia Hearst was formally imprisoned this total exposure of their writings was dramatically punctuated, as in Screed 11, with assertions that "failure to... print everything will endanger the safety of the prisoner."

The hapless Randolph A. Hearst, generously seconded by his colleagues on rival newspapers, and by many stations of the electronic media, leapt to meet the demand. His statement, made on February 12, was published in many, many places the following day.

We are, of course, taking the demands most seriously. We are doing all within our power to cooperate.

As requested, we will carry the letter in full in all editions of tomorrow's San Francisco Examiner.

We have also sought and obtained the cooperation of editors of other Hearst newspapers and of executive heads of Hearst radio and television stations. Thus, the full text will appear in the *San Francisco Examiner, Los Angeles Herald Examiner, Seattle Post-Inteiigencer, San Antonio Light, Baltimore News-American, Albany Times-Union, Albany Knickerbocker News Union-Star,* and *Boston Herald-American.* It will also be broadcast on WBAL AM-FM and WISN-TV, Baltimore, Maryland; WISN AM-FM and WISN-TV Milwaukee, Wisconsin, WTAE AM-FM and WTAE-TV, Pittsburgh, Pennsylvania, and WAPA Radio, San Juan, Puerto Rico.

These are the only newspapers, television stations and radio stations owned by the Hearst Corporation. There are, of course, more than 1700 newspapers and more than 2000 radio and television stations over which the Hearst Corporation exercises no power or control.

We have appealed to the owners of these stations and publications to cooperate to the greatest extent possible. We hope they will publish the text.

Counterscreed 4: HANG IN THERE, HONEY

Responding to Screeds 11, 12, and 13, which assured him that his daughter was still alive, but made the first impossible half-billion dollar demand upon his fortune, Randolph A. Hearst continued to take his soft line. The bumbling and apologetic tone which he adopted in this counterscreed of February 13, and in the news interview which followed it, was maintained until mid-April, when, in Screed 31, Patricia Hearst denounced him and he recognized that he had been tricked and cheated. The irony of his farewell phrase would not be evident until that later date.

Patty, I hope you're listening. We're really pleased to know that you're okay. You sounded a little bit tired or like you were sedated, but all right. And I'm sure the people who have you are telling the truth when they say they are treating you under the Geneva Convention.

I just want you to know that I'm going to do everything that I can to get you out of there. It's a little frightening because the original demand is what I was afraid of from the beginning, one that is impossible to meet.

However, in the next 24 to 48 hours I'll be trying my best to come back with some kind of a counter-offer that is acceptable.

It is very difficult because I have no one to negotiate with, except for the letters [here called screeds] which generally come two or three days later than we expect it.

Anyway, you can rest assured that Mother and I and all the family will do everything we can to get you out. Tell them not to worry. Nobody's going to bust in on them or start a shoot-out.

And take care of yourself. I think you'd like to know that everybody's praying for you. I think a few are even praying for the people that have you.

And we'd like to thank, and I'm sure you would like to thank, everybody who's rooting for you to get out of there and come home.

Hang in there, Honey!

Counterscreed 5: BIRTH OF THE COALITION

Screed 15, which conveyed the original demand for a free-food program, had listed fourteen race, radical, and counterculture groups as suitable to act as directors or referees. Most of these backed away at once. Others which came forward, hoping to help, included the Black Panther and Black Muslim organizations, and several integrated groups of ex-addicts, ex-prisoners, and the like.

Of the six organizations named in the screed, and agreeing to take part, the five most active were conspicuously Black. These were the Black Teacher's Caucus, the separatist Nairobi College of East Palo Alto, the United Prisoner's Union, the National Welfare Rights Organization, and Glide Memorial Church, headed by Cecil Williams. Faltering assistance was given by AIM, the American Indian Movement. In a February 13 meeting at Reverend Williams' Glide Church, leaders of the six groups agreed upon a joint statement registering their sympathy for Miss Hearst, agreeing to help with the food program, and tub-thumping on their familiar themes of inequality and social wrong. As shown in several screeds, with their headnotes, and in Counterscreeds 9 and 12, below, all six were soon to be overshadowed by Ludlow Kramer, Hearst's chosen PIN director, and then, more conclusively, by Arnold Townsend of WAPAC.

Currently the leader, Reverend Williams dominated in preparing the statement and in publishing it via newspapers and television. The special note on "distortion" refers to an AIM statement which had been regarded as too friendly towards tactics of the SLA.

The organizations represented here today are concerned with the welfare of the people in our communities. Our priorities are service and response to the needs and problems of our constituence. We feel strongly that any decisions to be made affecting them, must involve their participation and determination.

The groups represented here have no knowledge of the SLA. None of the organizations present today have been asked to participate in the demands of the SLA.

It is unfortunate that the needs and problems of the people hunger, racism, unemployment, sexism, ill heath, inadequate housing, injustice in our courts and prisons, the uneven distribution of wealth, and other inequities, which are a reality, receive public attention only when critical situations like this arise. Unfortunately, society does not look at the real problems of the people until confrontation occurs.

The oppressive conditions of our society are a reality, and the majority of the people with whom we work are poor and disenfranchised. However, we do not condone terrorist activity whether it is carried out by either the SLA or the Establishment.

We are concerned about the life of Patricia Hearst as we are about all human life. We are concerned about avoiding bloodshed in the case of both Patricia Hearst and the members of the SLA.

Therefore, we are willing to appoint representatives from our organizations to serve as a liaison between the Hearst family and the SLA, if doing so would provide a situation that will prevent further destruction of human life.

At this most critical time, we are appealing to the press not to distort or misrepresent any of these organizations' statements, as they did in the case of AIM's statement on February 12.

We do not want the life of anyone sacrificed. But the lives of numerous brothers and sisters who are held captive and have been threatened for years with death in prisons and communities across the country are equally important to us.

We here are all involved in organizations and movements fighting racism and inequity directed against the poor, the Third World, the welfare recipients, prisoners and ex-prisoners, the aged, the young, and all those who carry society on their backs. We are not capitulating on our goals and directions. We will continue to struggle for the freedom and self-determination of people in our communities. We will continue our struggle to remove oppression, unemployment; racism, and the social ills which destroy human life. But our goal is to organize and educate the people, to bring people together to create positive changes in their lives.

Counterscreed 6: A TOUCH OF PROPHESY

While the Hearsts contorted themselves in an effort to keep the Symbionese happy, and the press and police competed in low-keyed statements that the only object to work for was "to get Patty back," a few voices were raised in support of the theory of law and order. Conspicuous among these were Ronald Reagan's and William Saxbe's. As Governor of California, Reagan argued that the ordinary processes of law, justice, and social welfare were being distorted by SLA operations. An outspoken man, he confessed to a wish that the people who took the Hearst free food would be sickened by it. As the United States Attorney General, the nation's top prosecuting attorney, Saxbe uttered the sentiments recorded below. Any and all such statements were angrily rejected by Hearst and others as "antagonistic" and "irresponsible." But they were the statements that turned out to be right.

Saxbe's statement of February 21, 1974

America is now coming face to face with the problem we have seen in many areas of the world hijackings and political kidnappings. There is a worldwide trend toward terrorism which we are all aware of.

These terrorists will do just as much as they think they can get away with, and that is a problem that must be met head-on. They will be brought to justice. I don't think amnesty is an element in this. Certainly we would not be in a position to grant amnesty to any kind of a violent crime.

I personally feel that kidnapping and crimes that usually result from kidnapping are heinous crimes that should be covered by the death penalty. The deterrent to crime is the apprehension and prosecution of criminals, and I personally feel that nothing should stand in the way.

Counterscreed 7: WORD FROM BO AND OSCEOLA

The adventures of Russell Little and Joseph Remiro, or Osceola and Bo in the SLA nomenclature, can be traced in screeds and headnotes beginning with Screed 10, Fahizah's "Letter to the People." Moving out from the central characters of the Hearst drama, and flitting nervously from one short-lived star to another, the media eventually came to these two SLA soldiers, the accused murderers of Marcus Foster.

Little and Remiro, whose previous experience of prisons had only been theoretical, were now studying "prison conditions" from the inside. To protect them from other prisoners they had been moved from the Contra Costa County jail to security cells at San Quentin, and were waiting for transfer to the Alameda County jurisdiction in which they would be arraigned for the Foster murder. On the outside, meanwhile, the SLA screedspeople promulgated the theories of political imprisonment and "Geneva Conventions" which they had taken up immediately after the abduction of Patricia Hearst. Always in everybody's mind was the frightening idea that the welfare of Little and Remiro would be linked with the welfare, or even the life, of the captive girl.

To exploit this situation, Little and Remiro, with the help of one or more of their lawyers, began their own personal drive for attention and recognition. In Counterscreed 7 we find the captive soldiers at an early stage of this drive. Like so incredibly many others, they offer themselves as agents capable of assisting in negotiations between the Hearsts and the parent SLA. Going beyond that, they hint at the acceptability of a prisoner exchange, and exhibit the hypothesis that Patricia's real enemies are to be found in the FBI. In view of their fishbowl visibility at the time, their account of beatings and chokings at the hands of jail guards seems unlikely.

Their message arrived at Station KPFA, Berkeley, on February 27, and was read aloud on that and other stations. It was reported, but not reprinted, in newspapers. During the next few weeks their demand for public attention became more strident, and they appeared to be on the point of taking a management role in the conduct of affairs of the

case. In their next long message, given below as Counterscreed 10, they demanded that not only it but this preliminary message be printed in full; and the demand was duly met.

We, Joe Remiro and Russ Little, feel compelled at this time to expose to the general public the latest chain of events that we have experienced and the conclusions we have drawn from them.

First, we must give everyone some background information. We are being held in isolation, the Hole, on Death Row at San Quentin Prison.

The director of the California Department of Corrections, Raymond Procunier, has ordered this in an attempt to isolate us from news of what's happening on the streets and to keep the people on the streets from knowing what's happening to us. He is doing this under the direction of the FBI.

A prime example of this is the fact that last Tuesday, Feb. 19, Joe exposed the site of our present confinement, the oppressive visiting situation and the fact that we had not eaten any prison meals, since our forced move from the Adjustment Center, while in court in Martinez.

These statements and others made in the courtroom and also after court by our lawyers were completely suppressed by the news media.

Thursday, Feb. 21, at about 1:30 p.m., much to our astonishment, we got a phone call from our old friend "Death Row Jeff" Clifford Jefferson, a Folsom prison inmate. He explained that he was worried about us and had persuaded Procunier to allow him to call us and also arrange a meeting between the three of us Jeff, Joe, Russ.

At that point we asked that a lawyer be present at the meeting and agreed upon a lawyer to be contacted by Jeff immediately after our phone call was completed.

That same morning, Thursday, we had been discussing the vast coverage concerning the kidnapping of Patricia Hearst and the fact that this coverage has consistently included speculation that her safety and eventual release is linked to demands that we be released from custody.

In fact, the SLA has consistently referred to our safety and well being because they realize that we are innocent of the charges for which we are presently imprisoned!

We feel that a fair trial is virtually impossible anywhere in the United States. The speculative, biased, misinformative media campaign that has been waged against us has all but sentenced us to death!

We've concluded our discussion with a decision to try to come up with some suggestion that might be possibly be acceptable to the SLA, FBI and the Hearst family and which would result, if accepted, in the release of Patricia Hearst.

After finishing the telephone conversation with "Death Row Jeff," we knew the FBI had given Procunier their okay and speculated that their purpose would be to see if we had any viable suggestion to offer.

Later that night, at about 10:30 p.m., three guards came to our cells and told us we were leaving, destination unknown! After being shackled we were taken on a tour of the gas chamber, then placed in the back seat of a Department of Corrections car, where we remained for about one hour.

Still, no reason was given, but we decided that we were either going to meet with Jeff or be assassinated for an alleged escape attempt, since we were waiting outside of the actual prison walls!

Finally, we were driven to the first entrance gate and placed in an office across from the visitors waiting room. "Death Row, Jeff" arrived with Procunier and at least three carloads of FBI agents.

Jeff was brought into the room and we talked of our mutual concern for the Hearst woman and discussed a variety of suggestions. The meeting lasted from 12 midnight until 2 a.m.

Our demand for allowing a press conference, and the suggestions that we three agreed upon, were written down and handed to Procunier, who was acting as the go-between for the FBI and us.

We asked for nothing for ourselves and felt confident that, if Patricia Hearst's safety was primary with the FBI, they would set up the press conference. Joe and I also realized that the media's suppression of our status was a calculated power play to force us to participate in that meeting without any of our lawyers present.

After we woke up Friday, Feb. 22, we waited to be contacted by late afternoon. After hearing that Hearst was unable to meet the demands for an additional $4 million, we decided it would be best to try to get in touch with one of our lawyers and try to get the press conference together ourselves.

It was beginning to look, from the skimpy information we were getting, that a showdown was in the making. We sent word to Warden Nelson but he denied our request to phone a lawyer. We went all day Saturday and Sunday without any information on the kidnapping and without seeing or speaking to our lawyers.

Sunday afternoon, Feb. 24, at about three, we were taken from our cells, shackled and sent to the Alameda County maximum security jail. We arrived there at about 3:45 p.m. We were attacked about 15 minutes later by four deputy sheriffs during a strip search.

Both of us were beaten and choked. Russ sustained injuries to his left wrist, back, shoulders, neck and chest. He has been denied medical treatment and has had very little sleep since the attack because of pain. The officers also had spread rumors throughout the entire jail stating that we stabbed a black inmate at San Quentin with a knife supplied by a prison guard.

This racist lie was intended to cause us both verbal and physical attack by the prisoners. We refrained from mentioning this in court Monday Feb. 25. By this time, we realized, not only had the FBI refused to let us voice our suggestions but also they had decided to have us physically attacked in the hopes of retaliation by the SLA on the person of Patricia Hearst.

This latest chain of events, combined with our understanding of the corruption and ruthlessness of the Nixon Administration government, leads us to only one possible conclusion:

U.S. Atty. William Saxbe and the Director of the FBI, Clarence Kelley, want Patricia Hearst to die! They are desperately trying to discredit the SLA in the eyes of the nation's hungry oppressed people. We feel it is of utmost importance to expose this callous plan to the public in the hopes of averting the death of Patricia Hearst, those who are holding her, and ourselves!

We are asking the public to support our demand to be able to present our suggestions, and reasons behind them, to the SLA and the general public in a live nationally televised press conference.

A WARNING TO THE FBI:

Even if you kill us and or slaughter Patricia Hearst and those holding her, we have made provisions to ensure that our suggestions will be made public. Wednesday Feb.27

-Russ Little
-Joe Remiro

Counterscreed 8: REVOLT OF THE OAKLAND TRIB

As pointed out in the headnote to Counterscreed 3 and elsewhere, the often-repeated demand of the SLA screedspeople that their writings be published "in all forms of the media" was obeyed by all the significant papers of the Bay Area. Among those who bent over backward to oblige the SLA in this respect was the Oakland Tribune, the third of the Bay Area newspapers in size and significance. But after a month of printing the Hearst-kidnap documents, and three months of printing the Foster-murder documents, the Tribune rebelled. On March 10, in a special editorial statement, Joseph W. Knowland, the editor and publisher, pointed out that further compliance would not be forthcoming. The fourth-ranking Independent-Gazette of Berkeley, which had not followed the demand in any case, immediately associated itself with the decision.

As editor, I have issued a policy directive to The Tribune nullifying the SLA demand to The Tribune and other media to publish SLA communications in their "exact form, not omitting any area."

The SLA, the other media, the Hearst family, and some of the reading public may ask why. The following is my answer:

A Free Press is the keystone of all of your other basic freedoms granted by God and preserved and protected by our Constitution.

The SLA's extortion, placing tyrannical demands on the Hearst family, the public and the media alike, seeks to enslave us all the public as well as the press.

The "power of the press" and the "Freedom of the Press" carry with them "Responsibility." One of the primary responsibilities of the press is to PROTECT your remaining freedoms from any and all tyrants, be they governmental agencies, foreign powers or revolutionary organizations.

To Miss Patty Hearst, I say: If you are indeed alive, and are held captive, may God bless you and protect you.

To the Hearst family I say: May God give you the strength to survive this ordeal, and our prayers, hopes and empathies are with you.

To my colleagues in the news media, I say: NOW is the time to protect our country's freedoms, not "tomorrow." For if not "now," there will be no "free tomorrows."

To the SLA I quote Thomas Jefferson, who 174 years ago said it far more succinctly than I could: "I have sworn upon the altar of God eternal hostility against every form of tyranny over the mind of man."

Counterscreed 9: THE WAPAC REPORT, IF ANY

During the feverish free-food episode recorded in the middle screeds with their head-notes, the WAPAC neighborhood association led by Arnold Townsend had seemed to become the principal outside agent for the SLA, or at least for its programs. As spokesman for WAPAC and head of the so-called Coalition, Townsend had assumed media importance rivaling and finally surpassing that of Kramer, the head of the program. And Townsend, interpreting his duty as a policing and reporting one, had taken to speaking of a "WAPAC report" on the food transactions.

Listening from its secret places, the SLA leadership got the idea that the report was a written one, and that the printed media were demonstrating bad faith by failing to print it. Marshal Cinque and General Genina both had their say on this, for which see Screeds 17 and 19. "The SLA and the Court of the People," said the latter in her faked Black accents, "want to see the report printed in full in all forms of the media."

Scrambling to meet this demand, and still believing that Patricia Hearst might be returned if all SLA demands were met, the Examiner staff people "requested a copy of the WAPAC report, only to learn that it did not exist in written form." Townsend's talk, and nothing else, was the report. Moving to the electronic media, the Examiner people found that no complete statement by Townsend had been taped by television or radio stations. They finally found "the most complete recording of the Townsend-WAPAC report" in the record of a four-minute newscast carried on the Berkeley station KPFA, another of the SLA favorites.

The KPFA news report, with additions from Townsend and his cluster of WAPAC lieutenants, was duly printed in the Examiner of Wednesday, March 13.

KPFA's account of the conference opens with reporter Pat Roberto of KPFA saying—

Western Addition Project Area committee chairman Arnold Townsend reported today on yesterday's People in Need food distribution program. Re-emphasizing that his organization and other groups forming the coalition of observers were not in a position to judge the program itself or the decisions made by the People in Need organizers, Townsend made the following comments:

As a program, PIN is suffering from a lack of coordination between the directors and the community groups, which has resulted In the groups bearing a large part of the burden of the actual food distribution. For example, much of the responsibility for the transportation of food yesterday fell to the community organizations.

The coalition, said Townsend, came up with a different set of figures on the number of people served yesterday than did PIN officials. The coalition says that about 15,000 people were served, while PIN has said that about 28,000 got food.

There were other aspects in the implementation of yesterday's food giveaway which Townsend thought needed pointing out.

Arnold Townsend's voice is heard next, as he spoke at the news conference.

On Thursday, observing this lack of coordination, community observers took on the roles and responsibilities of enlisting volunteers and expediting the operation to insure that the lines of people at our doors would receive free food.

We believe that the community by its action in last Thursday's program shows its understanding for the necessity of high quality food distributed in a dignified manner.

And just to cite a few further examples of what we're talking about, in all eleven of the sites, there were only 44 PIN volunteers for packing the food and unloading the trucks, etc. Of those 44 PIN volunteers, 25 of these volunteers were at the Mission District Shotwell center. Which left 19 volunteers for the ten centers.

No centers received hams, as reported by some newsmen and some papers. It was our understanding they were going to be held until Saturday, and to our knowledge none went out.

Most centers did not receive bread nor fresh milk. Those that did, the supply ran out early.

Community people assumed most or all of the responsibility at the 11 centers. Deliveries were not on schedule and observers had to, in many cases, load trucks and that's at the warehouse and deliver them to their own communities.

Further, in reporting to the community, there are some points we should like to make clear. And that is that there were some policemen at the two West Oakland and the two Mission sites, traveling through the sites.

Another voice is heard (inaudible).

Townsend: And, excuse me, yes, at Fillmore.

Other voices shout names of other sites: And Hunter's Point Our place too—

Townsend: You see. Yes, West Oakland. However, there were no incidents or arrests. One incident in Oakland. The police came over and got some people who had broken into a place and gotten some bags that were there for the volunteers. And Mr. Johnson and his people went over and asked them told them to let them go. And they did let the people go.

Also, each bag contained about seven or eight dollars worth of food. Also, at each center, approximately 500 to 1000 people were turned away.

KPFA 's account concludes with a wrap-up by newswoman Roberto —

Townsend repeatedly denied that his report was any kind of an indictment of PIN director Ludlow Kramer or other organizers. "We are just stating facts as we perceive them," he said. And he would only add that, "We think there could be some improvements. They could do more of the things they say they are going to do." Townsend also said that he thought the new two-day-a-week schedule announced for the program by Kramer today might make the project more efficient. But he declined any opinion as to whether the shortened schedule would be acceptable to the SLA.

Counterscreed 10: FURTHER WORD FROM BO AND OSCEOLA

Following their first long letter, printed above as Counterscreed 7, Remiro and Little did most of their communicating through friends and lawyers, with the help of KPFA and other organs of the media.

In spite of the tense tragedy and low farce of ongoing transactions in the Hearst case, the East Bay wheels of justice managed to move a little, and the evidence that linked Remiro and Little to the Marcus Foster murder, and to lesser crimes such as arson, larceny, and shooting at policemen, began to come before an Alameda County grand jury. Rather than proclaiming their guilt as the SLA had formerly done, the captured soldiers now denied it. The rest of their indignant letter rehashes old themes. Patricia Hearst had not yet made her absolute juncture with the SLA and its vision of liberty and justice, but had done enough preliminary hinting to justify the friendly tone they adopt toward her.

To assist its being shown on television, Little and Remiro had carefully hand-printed their counterscreed in heavy capital letters, It was printed and read aloud in the various media on March 28 and 29. On the latter day, the two soldiers were indicted for the Foster murder, and other crimes.

We, Russ Little and Joe Remiro, have decided to go ahead and send out this statement instead of waiting for the live, televised press conference that we and our lawyers have exerted every effort to obtain. It should be obvious to all at this point, that those officials who interpret and enforce the laws are determined to stop the conference.

The news media have expressed support and offered to help get our statements out to the public. Now that it's not live let's see how many publish this statement in full and how many take excerpts out of context, as they did in our first statement, in an attempt to further prejudice people against us! If the news people are truly interested in informing the public, they will publish this statement and our first one, dated Feb. 27, in full:

As has consistently been the case since we were attacked and arrested on Jan. 10, the judges, D.A.s and sheriffs, with the supervision and support of federal law enforcement agencies, have conspired to keep us from speaking to the people. We asked for the press conference in the hopes of contributing to the safe and speedy release of Patricia Hearst! Why won't they let us speak? Patty says it herself, as does the S.L.A. in the last tape they sent out.

Briefly stated: the federal, state and local law enforcement agencies, courts included, are responding to the demands of the corporate powers whose interests they represent and protect at all costs! At this point they are so desperate that they would not even be completely satisfied with the death of those S.L.A. forces guarding her, or even the annihilation of the entire S.L.A. They seek to discredit the strategy and tactics of the S.L.A. and other revolutionary groups, and feel this can be accomplished only if Patricia is killed and her death blamed on the S.L.A.!! We realized this cold, brutal fact and discussed it at our midnight meeting, Thursday Feb. 21, with Death Row Jeff.

Procunier and those federal agents with him allowed Jeff and us to meet together in the hopes that, after a tour of the gas chamber, we would unconsciously aid them by just making a simple statement such as, "Release Patricia Hearst." Once they realized that we intended to expose their plan of action, they showed their true colors put Jeff in the "hole" in Vacaville, us in the "hole" in San Quentin, and tried like hell to stop us from communicating with the public. This racist, exploitive treatment of Death Row Jeff is typical of his prison experiences during the last 29 years and of the entire capitalist-imperialist system.

Another aspect of this meeting which seems to have been overlooked is, "Where did our hand-written suggestions go?

When we gave them to Procunier, he would not even look at them said they were for "higher-ups" (sounds familiar doesn't it?). The F.B.I. denied any participation or knowledge of the meeting, so, "Who read our suggestions? "Statements that no one knew what we intended to say are out-right lies!

People are expecting us to tell about the prison conditions we've encountered since our arrest. We've spent a little more than a month in San Quentin's maximum security, "adjustment center" and a few days short of a month in the "hole" on Death Row. In prison time this is hardly mentionable.

To find out about the "adjustment center" and the "hole" ask those who have spent precious years "locked down." Those who have been regularly and indiscriminately gassed and beaten with pick handles. Those who on Aug. 2, 1971, witnessed the murder of George Jackson. Those who have witnessed countless other murders in the name of "rehabilitation and adjustment."

Some have been beaten into insanity while others have been beaten into the objective reality which has led to the birth of organizations such as the B.G.F. and W.O.

Coblentz acting in the interests of the Hearst Corporation said that he visited us in the "hole" and was satisfied that we were being treated well. Our attorneys pointed out to the judge, in Alameda County, that such was not the case and requested that the judge personally view our conditions of confinement. The judge did as requested and immediately put out a court order to have us moved. This action must have taken some moral convictions but why is it that he or no other judge ever gave a second thought about two Black comrades who were also in the hole? At the time, they had been living under those same conditions for over 45 days, one of them without any hot water. We have learned that Elmer "Geronimo" Pratt is now also in the "hole" on Death Row. Why is it that Lt. Calley accused of killing many innocent civilians is out on a one thousand dollar "appeal bond," while Geronimo and other comrades have appeals also but no such "appeal bonds"? We question such moral convictions.

This is the same brand of morality that claims to put the highest of values on life, in respect to Patricia Hearst, and is silent while a C.I.A. sponsored, military dictatorship is murdering upwards of 80,000 innocent people in Chile. The same brand of morality that sits back while the U.S. government murders and supports the murdering of thousands of innocent human beings in Asia, South America, Africa, Ireland and all over the world. The same brand of morality middle class Amerikkkans use as they allow their government to carry out an organized terrorist campaign of murder and oppression in this country's ghettos, barrios, reservations and prisons. We have no respect for this brand of self-oriented, racist morality!

We do in fact, put the highest of values on human life all human life . This includes the life of Patricia Hearst as well as the lives of the children of the poor and oppressed peoples of the world. We do not hold Patricia Hearst responsible for the actions of the Hearst Corporation or the part it plays within the ruling class. We do, in fact, admire the level of courage and objectivity she has displayed and send her our warmest regards.

Patty, we feel that we have already done the most concrete thing we can do to assist in your safe release by exposing the true intentions of the F.B.I., etc. to the public. We feel confident that the S.L.A. will release you unharmed. We're glad to hear that you recognize the dishonest actions of your family in regards to meeting the food program and remaining silent while others jeopardize your safety. We hope that when you are released you will continue to be strong and speak your mind! We realize, as do you, that the S.L.A. has consistently referred to our safety and well-being but that in reality, you will not be harmed for anything that might happen to us. You're in no better position than us, as far as the reactionary force's intentions they want to make an example of your death as well as ours! Actually, you're in a better position only as long the S.L.A. can protect and keep you well hidden until you can be released and returned safely to your fiance. Who knows you might even look back on this as a worthwhile experience where people were fed and you and the public were exposed to the cruelty and inhumanity of the corporate powers who rule this country. It's good to hear you're reading George Jackson Soledad Brother is another beautiful book he wrote about the California prison system and the lives of nonwhite people in this country. We look forward to receiving a visit from you, Patty, after you are released.

To the Symbionese Liberation Army we also send our warmest love and regards. We understand the motivation of your actions, in our behalf, as you know that we are innocent and that there is no chance of us receiving a fair trial. Please don't waste your time or risk your lives worrying about us. We're in good health and spirits! Our struggle, at this time, is secondary. We join our comrades Lolita Lebron, Assata Shakur (slave name JoAnne Chesimard), Sundiata Acoci (slave name Clark Squire), Richaro Brown, Henry "Sha-Sha" Brown, the N.Y. Five and all those struggling from within these concentration camps, and expect our trials to also reflect the injustices of a sick society and oppressive system. We in no way feel isolated or surprised by the actions of the state and federal authorities. We are in unity with our comrades and grow strong in the realization that Comrade George [Jackson] lives.

We share the S.L.A.'s concern for the safety of Patty and the element guarding her. They are in grave danger and should deal with the primary tasks of the safe return of Patty to her fiance and the safe withdrawal of the S.L.A. element. We hope that "everyone" is preparing for the government's massive, terrorist assault that will surely follow Patricia Hearst's release. It's obvious that dozens of suspected S.L.A. members are now being actively sought. Once she is released many people and organizations will be attacked and put behind bars regardless of any guilt or knowledge of the S.L.A.! Just another fascist attempt to kill that which it breeds.

In ending we'd like to send a twit of our sincerest love and regards to the Black Guerilla Family. Weather Underground, Black Liberation Army and W. 0. and all other comrades. We'd also like to send our sympathies to all those intellectual, sunshine revolutionaries in a quote from George Jackson "If today's young revolutionary vanguard are not merely entertaining themselves with a new kind of chicken, a political form of bumper tag, if they seriously intend to step out front and take the monster to task, they should understand from the outset that the monster is merciless.

A Luta Continua — Venceremos
(The Struggle Continues — We Will Win)
Love — Joe Remiro, Russ Little

Counterscreed 11: BLA GREETS SLA

A small but deadly group of Black militants, the Black Liberation Army or BLA, soon expressed its appreciation of the SLA program. This terrorist group, usually estimated to have about 200 members, was more active in Eastern cities than in California. But one of its most exciting actions had been an armed attack on a San Francisco police station, and one of its members, Rubin Scott, was under indictment for the murder of a policeman killed there. Presumably the all Black BLA did not understand the predominately white and middle class membership of the SLA. In any case, the revolutionary greetings of BLA to SLA were duly mailed to the San Francisco Chronicle from a Berkeley mail box.

Profound revolutionary greetings.

Comrades in arms, we of the Black Liberation Army speak to you from our prison cells, our underground safe houses, from the streets and from the grave.

The dialectics of our conflicts has spiraled to the point of open guerilla warfare.

It is being waged against the number one enemy of mankind "The Military Armed Fascist Corporate American State."

We have been waging this protracted War of Liberation virtually alone. Oh but how sweet it is to hear the thunder of your weapons resounding on the battlefield.

We are coming of age. As the caterpillar becomes the butterfly, so the man-child becomes the armed combatant.

Counterscreed 12: FOOD AND POWER: A LAST WORD

As the Hearst or PIN food program guttered in dismay, shock, and finally grief, the so-called Coalition, which now titled itself "The People's Community Food Coalition," wrote its last report, which was also its first. The report follows the ordinary political strategy of denying virtue and energy to "administration" while loading these qualities on "the people" or "the community." It thus expands, almost to infinity, the hopelessly tangled tug-of-war that had developed between Ludlow Kramer and his do-gooder staff on the one side, and Cecil Williams, Arnold Townsend, and other skilled community politicians on the other. Its rising chords of praise to all private citizens and all "organizations with a community base" give emphasis to the practical fact that with the decline of Black church affairs, the Black leader's principal route to prestige, power, and tax-supported salaries has been through the politics of the "neighborhood" or the "community." Only when he was safe back in Washington State did Kramer declare that from first to last the PIN program had been mainly, in his words, "a power grab."

From: *Community Food Coalition*
To: *The Community*
Subject: *The People in Need Food Programs*

First we would like to state that this is and has been a very broad based coalition made up of the following organizations with food being distributed in the following areas:

1) East Oakland
2) West Oakland (Citizen's Neighborhood Assistance Program)
3) East Palo Alto (Nairobi College)
4) Richmond (Welfare Rights Organization)
5) Sonoma County Food Coalition
6) Vallejo — Original Americans of Vallejo
7) Marin City

SAN FRANCISCO

1. Chinatown
2. Western Addition
   a. Fillmore — WAPAC
   b. Haight — Haight-Ashbury Food Coalition
3. Hunters Point
4. Mission District
   a. United Prisoners Union
   b. Real Alternatives Program
5. South of Market
6. Potrero Hill
   Potrero Hill Community Government
7. Sunny dale
8. Double Rock

In areas where no organizations are named individual groups of people came forward to distribute the food. Also participating in the program were Glide Memorial Church, American Indian Movement.

We as a coalition were involved as observers and co-ordinators in the community end of the program. We were not responsible for purchasing, selection or transportation of the food, and have no power in, and can make no promises concerning, the wider events surrounding the food distribution program.

We feel that in any food distribution program such as this, people with organizing skills and a respect in the community should be involved at every level.

Administration: In the PIN program there was a general lack of coordination. There were no regularly scheduled meetings, charts, etc. There were no defined lines of authority or organization. Statements were made of a factual nature as to the coordination of the program and were later proven to be unfounded, such as in the areas of sites, volunteers, food, transportation. For example we were told that the program was ready to go with a ham in each bag, when in fact the hams were not even in California.

Volunteers: In regard to volunteers, PIN consistently exaggerated the number, i.e.: 4000. There was never the stated amount of volunteers in any center or in the PIN warehouse, this was another detriment to the distribution. In each distribution, in most cases except the last, community people had to go to the warehouse and load their own trucks.

Warehouses: Nowhere was the need for coordination more important than in the warehouse and nowhere was it more lacking. There was no system of checking what came in or the quantity of what came in. The program was lacking in quantity control, i.e., a large quantity of beef was ordered which was not up to standard. The pulling back of this beef created further disorganization and time loss.

Purchasing: The persons in charge were from out of state and had no knowledge of local supplies. They were inexperienced in appraising the quantity of food purchased and inexperienced in ordering food in the required quantity.

Distribution: Sites The selection, co-ordination and development of the sites was the responsibility of PIN. This task however ultimately fell on the community.

Transportation: The PIN administration failed on each distribution date to deliver trucks to chosen sites at designated times, which was one of the most vital parts of the entire operation.

Quality of Food Distributed: The food was accepted by the Community. According to a nutritionists report, requested by the coalition, the food was wholesome. The quality of the food improved with each distribution. Amount of Food Distributed: The amount of food varied from box to box. People were turned away at every site, at each distribution. As many people were turned away as were fed. The coalition repeatedly requested an accounting of the wholesale price of each box. We never received any such accounting. From time to time a count was made of the number of boxes to be distributed. These counts were made by various PIN officials, and often times were proved to be inaccurate and inconsistent.

Rip off: The problem rip-offs were internal with the PIN organization, from a combination of factors including poor warehousing, inefficient security, improper, purchasing practices, and poor administration.

The food was needed and welcomed by the people. However, it is a sad commentary that it takes an event such as this, to feed and illustrate the problems of the hungry. It was our feeling that the overall press coverage has done more to confuse the issues than to clarify them. For this reason it was requested that they not be present at the distributions and that is why there have been no recent press conferences by the coalition. The Community Coalition distributed food because we recognized that without the assistances of the coalition the distribution would be anarchistic and possibly harmful to our community. We also realized that the people needed it.

The coalition recognizes that in our practice criticisms can be made. We welcome and request that the community let us know these criticisms. There were very few uniformed police observed during the distributions although there were many in the vicinity. After the first attempted PIN distribution, it was clear that only organizations with a community base, can put a food program together with dignity and respect.

DARE TO STRUGGLE, DARE TO WIN, DARE TO LOVE!

Counterscreed 13: ONE OF THE BRAINWASH EXPERTS

After the conversion of Patricia Hearst to the life and principles of the SLA, great numbers of psychologists and psychiatrists stepped forward to explain. On the first was Dr. Frederick J. Hacker, a psychiatrist at the University of Southern California, who was consulted by the Hearst family and afterwards interviewed by the news media. We print an excerpt of the interview covered in the San Francisco Examiner of April 5, 1974, by reporter Gale Cook.

Patricia Hearst may have been brainwashed, an international expert on terrorism said today, but perhaps not so thoroughly that her captors can risk sending her home.

With $4 million hanging in the balance, Dr. Frederick J. Hacker asked, why didn't the Symbionese Liberation Army send Patty home to her family for a couple of weeks?

The fact that they didn't makes the University of Southern California psychiatrist believe that in the SLA's mind, at least, Miss Hearst is an uncertain convert.

Hacker described the technique that he calls "the dishonest productions of honesty" this way:

"If somebody is exposed to constant threat, not only to life, this then becomes a threat to his or her identity, to the full structure of formal belief, and this uncertainty can be cleverly manipulated to such an extent that even very strong persons think that they honestly change their mind."

There is at least good possibility that tactics like those made Patricia Hearst say she is joining the SLA, Hacker said.

Hacker, who has been consulted by the Hearst family in dealing with Patty's kidnappers, urged the public, to withhold judgment on the surface indication Patty has turned against her family.

Hacker said publicly on March 4 that the cheerful tone of Patty's voice in the second tape indicated she was reacting to danger by adopting some of her captor's viewpoints.

He pointed out that in some hijacking cases, stewardesses had established a quasi-love relationship with the hijackers and later were reluctant to testify against them.

Concerning Miss Hearst's most recent statement, Hacker said:

"There is the possibility, as I predicted, that by clever manipulation, spontaneously a kind of sympathetic relationship develops with the underdog, and that furthermore this kind of relationship can be manipulated.

"I would urge, until we have full disclosure of what happened, that the community look at this thing with a great deal of caution and charity.

"We know from experience with American prisoners in Korea and China that clever brainwashing can lead to surprising results.

"This is possibly the most dangerous threat of modern technology and modern psychology that free consensus can be manipulated.

"Coercion can wind up as a consensus that appears to be free, can lead to psychological changes causing a decision seeming to be totally free while in fact it is a result of coercion."

Systematic coercion, he emphasized, can in a case like Patricia Hearst's produce the semblance of freedom even for the subject herself

"We know again from scientific experience that if total input of information is controlled, guided and censored, that you can in a large number of people produce very important changes of mind," Hacker said.

"This has been the whole experience in the totalitarian system. It's no coincidence that in Russia most people are Communists.

"Therefore if that has taken place, Patty or a person in that position deserves sympathy and charity rather than censure and rage."

Hacker said he did not rule out the additional possibility Miss Hearst
was simply compelled to make her statement by crude force. However, he thought this less likely.

Hacker is a professor on the faculty of USC medical school and of the USC law center. His most popular class is a law course in the tactics of terrorism.

Counterscreed 14: REVOLUTION UNDER CONSTITUTION

At the beginning of May, when a San Francisco grand jury finally began to hear evidence about the newer crimes of the SLA, it called in a number of witnesses. Most of these belonged to radical and revolutionary circles in the Bay Area, and some had been intimate with SLA members even after the organization turned to its program of "actions." Most had already refused to assist the police, and some now refused to assist the grand jury. In their statements, they almost invariably asserted that in being called on to give evidence, they were being denied rights insured to them by American law and the American Constitution. Paul L. Halverson, 27, had already refused to help the FBI, as his counterscreed will indicate. He now denies the legal right of the Grand Jury to question him. The National Lawyers' Guild which he mentions is a radical group set up by Marxists in the 1930's, and currently active in liberal and left causes of all sorts.

At the outset, I wish to publicly state that I have no connection with the SLA. I have no information that I can provide the grand jury that the FBI does not already know.

Our subpoena apparently springs from the fact that my wife and I are friends of Camilla Hall. The last communication we received from her was a brief note several months ago. The FBI has already obtained this from us by a ruse.

We have learned (from our attorney and a National Lawyer's Guild publication on grand juries) that the questioning of witnesses in grand jury proceedings can take any form the government prosecutor wishes it to take. They can ask a witness virtually any question they want, even if it has nothing to do with the matter being investigated.

I am an American citizen and a veteran of the Vietnam war.

I was raised to believe that I lived in the greatest country in the world because we had the Constitution and the Bill of Rights to guarantee us our freedom that could not be taken away by any government But now I have encountered "Catch 22," the grand jury.

During grand jury proceedings a witness' Constitutional rights are suspended and he or she is expected to answer any and every question presented to them by the government prosecutor or be found in contempt.

To be found in contempt is to be sentenced to spend the remaining term of the grand jury behind bars, which could be a sentence of up to 18 months. My attorneys and I have agreed we will resist this violation of my constitutional and legal rights by every means at our disposal.

If we are to remain a free country, then the American people must be made aware that threats to our individual liberties are on the increase. Our Democratic form of government is deteriorating, witness the whole Watergate affair. Our individual freedoms are being threatened, witness grand jury proceedings.

The founders of this nation were interested in keeping governments in the hands of the people, and I am sure that if Thomas Jefferson, Benjamin Franklin, and George Washington were around today they would be horrified by the slogan that has appeared of late: "America Love it or Leave it."

Power corrupts, that is a well known fact, and keeping America free requires the continued effort of all its citizens, of all political persuasions. We cannot merely say "the government knows best," because whether we like it or not, that means we are giving up what our founding fathers had in mind that we, the people, should be the government.

The Right and the Left need each other if we the people are to maintain control of this government.

I have committed no crimes against the state or any individuals within the state; and if I end up in jail as a result of these grand jury proceedings, it will be because I refused to relinquish my Constitutional rights.

Paul L. Halverson

Counterscreed 15: A LAST SCHEME OF DEATH-ROW JEFF

Clifford Jefferson, a Black robber and murderer serving a life sentence in the Vacaville prison, had already tried to intervene in favor of the SLA by working toward an exchange of Patricia Hearst for Little and Remiro. His attempted intervention is acknowledged in Tania's Screed 28. When Patricia became Tania, and the SLA gave up the idea of exchange, it also gave up the idea of ransom. As April drew on and that plan withered, Jefferson noted that time was running out on the four million dollars held in escrow against the release of Patricia Hearst. He then developed a new plan by which the money could be saved for "the poor and the people." As a by-product of phone calls exchanged with Randolph A. Hearst, he taped his new plea to his revolutionary comrades outside the walls. Media published his counterscreed on May 1 and May 2. There was no SLA response, and the four million went out of escrow and back to the Hearst Corporation at midnight of May 3.

My name is Clifford Jefferson. I am called by my friends Death Row Jeff. I am speaking to my comrades of the SLA, especially to the combat unit. I would like to first extend my very personal greetings to all the poor and oppressed people of the world. Also, I would like to extend a very warm personal greetings to General Field Marshal Cinque, and to all our combat forces in the field. Likewise, I would like to extend greetings to two of my close comrades, Russ Little and Joe Remiro, and not forgetting [prison friends] Albert Taylor and Raymond Scott.

Now, Cin, the reason I'm talking to you here now is because I personally believe that you have did something that no other revolutionary in the United States has done, and I say it to a multitude of people. I am sure that you are aware that there is many, many poor and homeless [sic on all errors] to be fed, and I am sure also that you realize that in the last communique from myself and Ray Scott and Al that it was a deadline mentioned that came into $4 million dollars in escrow to feed the poor and homeless people. And this deadline expires May 4. [Actually May 3] I have complete confidence in you, Cin, in every respect. I have complete confidence that you will do what is proper in every respect, for sure, that these other poor and oppressed people be fed.

Further, I would suggest that there is no doubt in my mind whatsoever that Comrade Tania freely and voluntarily joined the SLA. I know she was not brainwashed and I know she is completely dedicated to the people. I realize that she was accused along with many other beautiful comrades of being involved in a people's action in robbing the bank. But it's my belief that Comrade Tania would better serve SLA above ground, go around the country and around the world teaching to the people, talking with the people. Let the peoples know what SLA's goal is, and what SLA stands for, and the love and duty of every SLA member.

So, think about this, Comrade Cin. I hope you will respond as soon as possible to this, Comrade Cin. I know that it'll be difficult for Comrade Tania for a few days, but I've been assured that she will be permitted to speak freely in behalf of SLA, where I think she will best serve. With this, I am saying love and struggle, with my personal and very personal greetings to you, Comrade Cin.

Hello, comrade forces. Dare to struggle and dare to win!

FURTHER READING

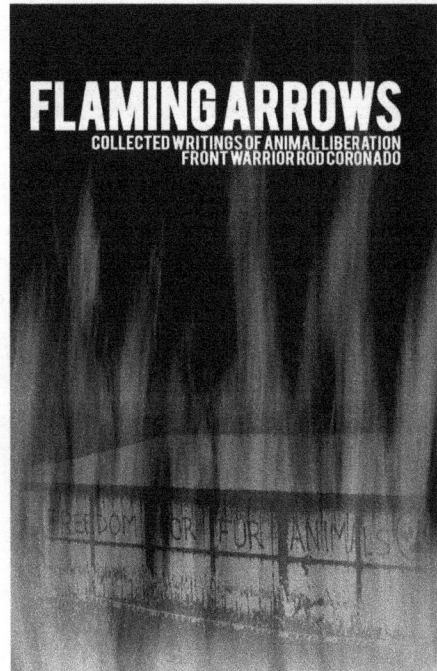

LIBERATE
STORIES & LESSONS ON ANIMAL LIBERATION ABOVE THE LAW

PETER YOUNG

ANIMAL LIBERATION FRONT
COMPLETE DIARY OF ACTIONS

Peter Young, Editor

UNDERGROUND
The A.L.F. IN THE 1990s

FLAMING ARROWS
COLLECTED WRITINGS OF ANIMAL LIBERATION FRONT WARRIOR ROD CORONADO

ALF STrIKES AGAIN!

THE A.L.F. STRIKES AGAIN

COLLECTED WRITINGS OF THE NORTH AMERICAN ANIMAL LIBERATION FRONT

Edited by Peter Young